10 SACRED
Questions
FOR EVERY WOMAN

*About Love, Friendship,
and Finding True Happiness*

JULIE GOHMAN, PH.D.

10 Sacred Questions for Every Woman
Copyright © 2015 by Julie Gohman

All rights reserved. Printed in the United States of America.
No part of this book may be used or reproduced in any manner
whatsoever without written permission except in the case
of brief quotations embodied in critical articles,
reviews, or books.

Clearwater Publishing House

For information please visit **www.juliegohman.com**

Book and Cover design by Derek Murphy.

ISBN: 978-0692393451
0692393455

First Edition: January 2015

10 9 8 7 6 5 4 3 2 1

Dedication

This book is dedicated to all my sisters

To the young women of today.
May you never silence your voice
But roar loud and wild and free.

To the mothers of the world.
May you learn to nourish your true self
As you nourish others so lovingly.

To the grandmothers throughout time.
May you guide us with your wisdom
Because we need it now more than ever.

To the daughters of the future.
May you be both bold and fearless
So you can spread your wings and soar.

Acknowledgments

Every chapter in this book has many unnamed contributors—friends, family, and colleagues—who provided rich insights into the nature of womanhood. Each sacred question reflects the experiences of not only myself, but also many women who have been brave and honest enough to reveal their depths to me.

I have been fortunate to have help from a team of talented and trustworthy people, each of whom added immeasurably to the development of this book. Thank you to Dara Beevas, publishing consultant, Derek Murphy, cover designer, and Rebecca Metz, social media expert.

My family has been a steadfast source of support as I labored on this book. My husband, Bret, and my two children, Sam and Andy, have given me the time and space and understanding that I needed to complete this project. I am grateful to be surrounded by a wonderful network of family and friends who have encouraged me every step of the way.

Contents

Dedication iii
Acknowledgments v
Preface ix
Introduction xiii

The First Sacred Question
What Would I Do If I Were Not Afraid? 1

The Second Sacred Question
What is My Soul Story? 21

The Third Sacred Question
Am I Ready For Wabi Sabi Love? 42

The Fourth Sacred Question
What Is True For Me? 66

The Fifth Sacred Question
How Can I Bring The Wild Feminine Alive? 82

The Sixth Sacred Question
Do I Have The Gift Of True Friendship? 101

The Seventh Sacred Question
What Is My Body Trying To Tell Me? 116

The Eighth Sacred Question
Am I Ready To Dance With The Moon? 135

The Ninth Sacred Question
How Can I Fill My Life With Ecstasy? 152

The Tenth Sacred Question
What Do I Need To Flourish? 168

Epilogue: The Most Powerful Question of all 187

Suggested Reading List 201

About Julie Gohman 209

Preface

*Learn to get in touch with the silence within yourself and
know that everything in this life has a purpose, there are
no mistakes, no coincidences, all events
are blessings given to us to learn.*
—Elisabeth Kübler-Ross

Inside each one of us there is a source of wisdom, a powerful presence that leads to a happy and beautiful life—if we are but willing to turn within and listen to its voice. An inscription carved into the temple at Delphi thousands of years ago expressed this idea simply and eloquently: "Know thyself." Self-knowledge is the foundation for all else—it is the key that unlocks the door to an authentic and meaningful life. And it is our deepest soul-searching questions, the ones that lead us into the shadows, that eventually help us shine our brightest light.

This book is an invitation for women to venture into the process of self-inquiry. It is for every woman who has ever lost her way, or lost her true self. It is for every woman who has found herself restless and yearning. Here you will explore the wellspring of love and wisdom that comes from within.

If you are ready to dive deep under the surface, into the landscape of the soul, keep reading. If you seek to understand the secret rhythms of your life, turn the page. If

Julie Gohman, Ph.D.

you are hungry to feel alive with womanly soulfulness—the kind that is complete and wholehearted, filled with dancing and laughing and loving—you have come to the right place.

The quality of every woman's life reflects the quality of the questions she is willing to ask herself. Questions are like seeds. Some questions feed new life. Some questions must be planted for us to grow. Others must be answered for us to blossom and flourish.

It is only when we go within, and ask well-crafted questions that we can create a life that we love. The most powerful and enduring transformations in a woman's life come when she experiences a shift from the inside. When that happens, we begin to live from the inside out, and bravely begin following our inner compass—one step, and one sacred question, at a time.

It is only when we go within, and ask well-crafted questions that we can create a life that we love.

A question becomes sacred when it invites personal transformation by opening our mind and heart to the greater mysteries of life. There are many good ways to ask sacred questions, and there is great wisdom in the act of questioning itself. Any inquiry that serves as a call of awakening is sacred.

Spiritual traditions offer many pathways to awakening and transformation. Some practices use breath to quiet the mind and open the heart while others use mantras, rituals, meditations, prayers, devotional chants, or drumming and dancing. We can spend time in nature. We can sit by trees or immerse ourselves in water (my personal favorites). The important thing is to open to the greater mystery and begin asking questions.

Pathways will form between the questions we ask and the answers that come—from the soul, from God, from the angels, from the divine. All of these pathways will lead to becoming receptive and open. When we open ourselves to the mystery we learn that wisdom is always available to us and in fact, surrounds us and infuses us. An inner voice speaks when we are willing to listen.

We do not open ourselves to the mystery just to get answers—we do it in order to move beyond the self to something greater. Whether we call that greater something our higher power, Great Spirit, God or Divine Love, it reflects the great ocean of life that sparkles with light. We are complicated and astonishingly diverse creatures, but underneath our differences we all partake of the divine, and it is pure, good, and beautiful.

*Every woman has a story to tell—
it is the story of becoming her true self.*

Every woman is on a journey to discover her *own* sacred presence. Our sacred presence is our authentic, true, inner self. I believe that women do have a quest at this time in our world. It is the quest to fully embrace our feminine nature, and to learn how to value ourselves as women. Every woman has a story to tell—it is the story of becoming her true self.

A longing to transcend disenchantment and emptiness is a call to the adventure of discovering our true self. It is not by sailing away on the high seas that women find themselves. Learning how to be true to our soul is the real adventure—with ceaseless rounds of questions and answers, spoken, lived, and felt.

Women find the strength and resilience to be their best selves in the down and dirty messiness of real life. It is here that women are living out their spiritual quests for goodness, meaning, and truth. One of the great lessons from the mystics in all spiritual traditions is that the sacred is in the ordinary. Everyday life is where we love and grow and learn what it means to be a woman.

There is a profound truth on the spiritual path for every woman. Like an intricate spider's web, every strand of a woman's life is part of the beauty that is woven into the grand design. We can trust that wherever we find ourselves, and whatever we are facing, our situation is meant to awaken us to the wisdom that resides within. There is wisdom that comes from our joy, and wisdom that comes from our sorrow. Both are pathways to truth.

Sometimes harsh circumstances bring us our most valuable lessons. Pain and turmoil bring a rawness that intensifies our desire to understand our purpose for living. The crises in our life inevitably reveal how impossible it is to control our destiny. At some point, every woman finds herself mired in disappointment and disillusionment, fighting against what is. The gift in these periods of time is the humility and compassion that grows when we struggle, and how honestly we begin to question everything.

Have faith that when you whisper a question and listen, as the Quakers say, "Way will open."

Every sacred inquiry begins wherever we find ourselves. Whether you are young or old or somewhere in between, it is never too soon or too late to begin understanding yourself better. There is no better time than right now to begin asking sacred questions. Have faith that when you whisper a question and listen, as the Quakers say, "Way will open."

Introduction

*If you want peace upon earth first establish
peace in your heart.
If you want union in the world, first unify the different
parts of your own being. Change yourself and the
circumstances will change.*
—The Mother

Not long ago, I stood with my family at the foot of my paternal grandmother's grave. Her name was Rosella, but we called her Grandma Babe. Her gravestone is small and lodged in the earth, edged with grass. It is one among many, marking the life of a remarkable woman. I stood there in the cold that day, surrounded by a heavy silence. We were all lost in our own thoughts and memories. I found myself staring at the worn letters of my grandma's name, and the dates that marked her short life. Images flooded my mind of her big warm smile, and her body bent over in the hot sun tending her garden, the way she wrapped her arms around me and held me close. Tears started to trickle down my cheeks.

I only know snippets of her story, small pieces of information that my father relinquished when I prodded him. But they are enough. I know that my Grandma Babe was a strong woman and a loving mother. I know that when she was faced with broken dreams and hardship, she didn't give

Julie Gohman, Ph.D.

in or give up. She kept going, kept loving, kept working, and kept laughing. Instead of growing bitter or apathetic about her circumstances, she chose to embrace life—in all its beauty and tragedy—with an open heart. She did not let what happened to her define who she was. As Elizabeth Kübler-Ross said, "The most beautiful people we have known are those who have known defeat, known suffering, known struggle, known loss, and have found their way out of the depths. These persons have an appreciation, sensitivity, and an understanding of life that fills them with compassion, gentleness, and a deep loving concern. Beautiful people do not just happen."

In a moment of silliness, my friend Nana nicknamed me the Question Queen. It is true, I was one of those kids that never stopped asking questions, much to my parent's irritation. And yes, I still probably ask too many questions (I am sure my family would love to duct tape my mouth shut during movies), but I have come to see life as one gigantic question mark. I believe we must learn to question everything boldly, fearlessly, and unabashedly. We must peer into those wild places that scare us. We must go there to find all the lost pieces of ourselves.

Life is an eternal process of seeking and finding, asking and answering, creating and dissolving, and living and dying. As women, we are constantly examining ourselves, and the questions we ask evolve quite naturally as we change. What concerns us in our 20's is very different than what captures our attention in our 40's, and that continues to change as we turn 50 and then 60 and enter new stages of womanhood. I laugh when I look back and remember what I fretted about ten years ago. How silly it seems now. Through it all, however, there will always be universal questions about who we are, what we are meant to do, and what life is truly about. Every woman wonders about her worthiness, and wants to be loved and appreciated. Every woman wants to have purpose, meaning and passion.

Sometimes we receive answers before we have even asked the questions. The process of inquiry is not always linear and sequential. At a recent workshop, a participant told me about a time when she was taking a morning walk and heard a intriguing sound off in the distance. Her intuition told her to follow it. After a few minutes she came upon a small waterfall that was hidden from the road. As she looked at the water softly splashing down the hillside and around the rocks, she thought of her grandfather, whom she had been close to all her life. "My grandfather's love is like that waterfall, always streaming down upon me in a peaceful, quiet way." she said. "I could feel his presence. And then I knew, that was my answer to the question: Why was my grandfather so special to me?"

"May you experience each day as a sacred gift woven around the heart of wonder."

Like the tumbling pieces in a kaleidoscope, different aspects of who we are come into focus at different times in our life. New questions pop into our minds at different moments. Answers come to us in unexpected ways. A hawk flies overhead and you feel a premonition, an inspiring passage comes to you during a difficult time, or a friend shows up just when you need her most. These things may seem ordinary—but they are moments of synchronicity that are meant to help us along the way. They are gifts. As one of my favorite authors, John O'Donohue wrote, "May you experience each day as a sacred gift woven around the heart of wonder."

Everything that happens in our lives brings us closer to what it is we need to discover—life is not happening to us, life is happening for us—even if it doesn't seem like it at the time. There is something to learn from every situation. Every day gives us new opportunities. We are either living more fully or withdrawing into less. We can either work with our life circumstances or struggle against them. We can either succumb to our fears or face them in the light of truth. As we develop more confidence, everything will improve. Even if our stomach is doing flip-flops, we can learn to say what we need to say. When things aren't going well, we can take a deep breath and relax—knowing there is something greater than us at work.

This I know for sure—the most difficult times in a woman's life are not when others do not understand her, it is when she does not understand herself. Our tendency to give ourselves away is perhaps why our relationship with our own true self suffers so greatly. As much as we try to understand and love others more deeply, much of what we go through as women is learning how to offer compassion and acceptance to ourselves—just as we are.

What I have found is that many women are yearning, but for what, they sometimes do not know. Something inside of them is breaking open. Something that was swallowed up and forgotten about long ago wants to be set free. There is a longing to rediscover oneself, a drive towards transformation, and a need to find purpose and meaning. We are being invited to dream bigger and shine brighter. It is a tumultuous yet exciting time in a woman's life. We are being led to the divine within us, and entering the landscape of heart and soul.

Who am I?
Why am I here?
What is the purpose?

At some point in our lives we all begin asking the perennial questions: Who am I? What is my purpose? What do I really, really, really want? Where do I belong? What is my legacy? We want to have that deep sense of being fully present and alive—to find meaning and purpose and do what is true to our soul, true to our essence. According to Joseph Campbell, the great mythologist, *that* is the definition of *bliss*. Getting there requires us to trust that when we are inspired, mysterious forces and dormant talents come alive in us. We discover that we are far greater, and that life is more beautiful and satisfying, than we ever dreamed it could be.

Like the legendary bird from mythology, the Phoenix, we have to be willing to let some things die away so that we can rise from the ashes reborn. It is an act of courage that no one else can do for us. We must begin listening more with our heart and less with our ears. Learning how to become comfortable with the uncertainty of life is part of the journey. Eventually we come to realize that life is *now*, and now is all we truly have.

Where is my power?
What do I believe?
What now?

We have all experienced times of disequilibrium and change. Often, we discover we are completely unprepared to deal with it, even though we perhaps knew it was coming all along. Divorce, disaster, disease, disappointment, death—there is nothing like personal experience to teach us life's greatest lessons. The anger, hopelessness, grief, and pain we experience may lead us to the questions that prompt us to stretch and grow. Questions such as: What can I learn from this situation? How can I nourish my health and well being?

Julie Gohman, Ph.D.

How can I stay calm and peaceful? Where is my power? What do I believe? What now? We all have spiritual work to do. Therefore, it is necessary to ask questions that help us release what no longer serves us, and make choices that are filled with integrity and authenticity, choices filled with honor, love, and respect. It becomes the work of a lifetime, if not many.

Rediscovering my true self has been a spiritual journey—not always easy, but totally worthwhile. As Marianne Williamson writes, "Spiritual growth is like childbirth. You dilate, then you contract. You dilate, then you contract again. As painful as it all feels, it is a necessary rhythm for reaching the ultimate goal of total openness." Becoming who we are is an ongoing process, not a final destination.

*Life is an adventure
of peeling away illusions
and discovering deeper truths.*

Asking sacred questions with an open mind and heart is part of discovering the beauty and wisdom that lives within us, and all around us. Little children do this wonderfully. They are curious and open and ask a million questions about everything. We would do well to rediscover our ability to wonder, explore, and play with what we know because we are in a continual process of transformation, individually and collectively. Opening our minds and hearts is how we discover who we really are; our "whole" self is free to emerge. Paying attention to our wholeness means we attend to six core areas of our life:

- *Intellectual*
- *Emotional*

- *Spiritual*
- *Physical*
- *Social*
- *Creative*

My values have shifted as I have learned to embrace my wholeness. I now live with more mindfulness, compassion, discernment, peacefulness, and unity. These are values that have given me the courage to become who I am—while at the same time honoring and appreciating the experiences of others. In many ways, it is like putting together a puzzle and finding all the delightful pieces of who we are. The quest for wholeness requires time, patience, and thoughtfulness. As we come to know ourselves better, we learn to make choices with care. These life choices reflect our growing inner wisdom and lead to joy and well being because they honor who we are.

One of our most important tasks in life is to continue learning from everything that happens to us, to discover the true gold that lies within every situation. Life is an adventure of peeling away illusions and discovering deeper truths. As the poet Rainer Maria Rilke wrote, "Be patient toward all that is unsolved in your heart and try to love the questions themselves…the point is to love everything. Live the questions now. Perhaps you will then gradually, without noticing it, live along some distant day into the answer."

Use these 10 sacred questions like a treasure map that will lead you to one of the best gifts you could ever give or receive: your most radiant and true self. The questions are in random order; one is not more important than another. Read the book as you wish (I sometimes start at the back myself). There are blank journal pages at the end of every chapter. They are for you, dear friend. Take a few precious moments and ask yourself the sacred questions in whatever way feels best. Go within, and then use these pages to write, draw, and express whatever you discover. May you have the courage to ask yourself these 10 sacred questions in the spirit of love and compassion, the kind you would offer to your very best friend. May you be blessed on your sacred journey of womanhood.

Remember the words of Rumi, the 13th-century Persian poet, who said:

> *"Everything in the universe is within you.*
> *Ask all from yourself."*

1

The First Sacred Question

What Would I Do If I Were Not Afraid?

Reach high, for the stars lie hidden in your soul.
Dream deep, for each dream precedes the goal.
—Mother Theresa

Imagine there are only two shoe boxes in your closet. Hard to imagine, I know—I love shoes too. One box is full of all the things you would like to happen in your life. This box is filled with positive thoughts, joyful emotions, success, prosperity, love, excitement, and dreams come true. The label on this box isn't Gucci or Jimmy Choo; it is "I can." The shoes from this box slip onto your feet like magical slippers. They are comfortable, elegant, and perfectly you! You can do anything in these shoes. The other box is filled with what you do not want to happen in your life. This box is filled with fear, negativity, doubt, worry, indecision, and criticism. The label on this box says, "I cannot." The shoes in this box are too small. They pinch your toes, and they're not your style. You can hardly walk in them, much less run or dance.

Now think about which box you would rather open. Think it over carefully. Every time you fear something, you are opening the box with the shoes that are too small for you. You are walking around with blisters on your feet and probably complaining about how much pain you're in. Your fear thoughts aren't wrong, but they are limiting you. These shoes are preventing you from being your true self and creating the life you want. The secret is—you are the only one who can take the uncomfortable shoes off.

When you want to focus on shedding fear, think about opening the box that is filled with positive thoughts and joyful emotions, the one labeled "I can." Put on the shoes that feel like magical slippers. Now you can create anything. Passion and possibility create excitement. Fear falls away. When you open this box, your vision expands and you feel wonderful about your life. The key is —you are the one who must ultimately accept that you are worthy of comfortable shoes that are just as beautiful as you are.

What is fear?

Fear is the cheapest room in the house said Hafiz, the Persian poet. You are not here on this earth to live in fear— you deserve so much better. How do you know when you are experiencing fear? You feel the impulse to run away and protect yourself, or you clam up and try to put a shell around the parts of you that are vulnerable.

> *You are not here on this earth to live in fear—*
> *you deserve so much better.*

Some fears are protective. There are times we must anticipate danger to survive. Judith Orloff, M.D., author of *Positive Energy*, writes that trustworthy intuitions will energize us whereas irrational fears will exhaust us. When you get a gut feeling that something isn't right, trust it, or at least slow down and reassess the situation. However, irrational fears that sap our energy are often personally demeaning and lack that gut feeling confirmation. Sometimes, even though we know our fears are irrational we just can't shake them. As Judith says, "fear grips your spirit and just won't let go."

How do you know if fear has a hold on you? You will feel a heaviness in your heart, confusion in your mind, and tension in your body. Fear may show up as worry, concern or grief. Instead of feeling joyful and light, you feel depressed, and powerless. Instead of being a self-protecting mechanism, fear can turn into a way of life. When you are living in fear, the world becomes a threatening place. And when you feel threatened, you cannot live with an open heart. When your heart is locked away, you are living in a tomb of despair and the energy of fear keeps you from growing and making positive, life-giving changes.

When you have a lot of fear, you naturally try to create a world that feels more safe and predictable. As you try to control everything in order to avoid your fears, life becomes a struggle—because life is a chaotic and deeply creative adventure that is fundamentally unpredictable.

The opposite of fear is freedom, letting go, trusting life, and opening your heart.

The opposite of fear is freedom, letting go, trusting life, and opening our heart—again and again. When fear has no hold over you, you discover the kind of happiness that is unshakeable. You become willing to face everything and everyone with honesty, courage, and openness. You learn to let go of the pain and sorrow that fear causes. When fear no longer dominates your life, you are ready to begin the journey to your true self—the journey to discover the brilliant, talented, and fabulous woman you were born to be.

True self

Our true self is that part of us that is connected to, and part of, the divine. Some may also refer to it as our heart, spirit, or soul. Our true self is the pure essence of who we are, and it calls us to our destiny. Our true self knows no limits and dwells only in possibilities. When we are in harmony with who we really are we radiate light and love and healing. There is no fear when we are living from our true self. When we love and trust the pure essence of who we are, fear fades away because we know the unshakeable truth—we are smart, strong, creative, and beautiful women.

As little girls, we start out strong in our soul selves.

As little girls, we start out strong in our soul selves, however, as we grow older, the limiting ideas of others stifle our intuition, instincts, and freedom of expression. We are often taught by generation after generation of self-sacrificing mothers and grandmothers that our success, happiness, and creativity are optional. Perhaps we are raised to believe that life is difficult and that this world is a frightening place to be for women. We may have been conditioned to believe that because we are female we cannot make it on our own. Unconsciously, we begin to shame and blame ourselves, thinking we are not good enough, or smart enough, or pretty enough. Some of us react by setting out to prove everyone wrong. We become the super-achievers of the world, trying to show everyone how smart and successful we really are. However, many of us learn to fear life itself. This fear causes us to silence our soul voice and doubt our inner wisdom. Indeed, by the time a girl reaches adolescence, if she has not been taught to be strong and confident, she will have, to a large extent, been robbed of her spirit. As women, when our true self is forced underground, our dreams, hopes, and creativity lose their momentum, and we lose our way.

But this is changing. Women are learning how to change their consciousness so that self-love and self-worth are replacing the fear that has taken hold, and in doing so, life becomes an experience of abundance and freedom. This is a giant leap forward for women. As women continue to shatter the limitations of previous generations, we are discovering there is nothing we cannot overcome when we wake up to our greatness. There is nothing we cannot achieve when we release the fear that is holding us back.

*There is nothing we cannot overcome
when we wake up to our greatness.*

When fear takes the wheel, we learn how to stay very busy in our outer life. We rush around, hiding under the guise of *doing* rather than *being*. We dutifully put aside our needs, and buy into what is called the "disease to please." Most women spend years trying to overcome this madness that chips away at our soul. We succumb to the demands of all sorts of time bandits without realizing the true cost to our life. Motherhood, marital bliss, and professional success often come at the expense of our physical, mental, and emotional health. The energy vampires bleed us dry when we are not vigilant about setting boundaries and protecting our life force.

Although most women have become adept at suppressing their true self and neglecting their own needs, this can only go on for so long. When our true self is ignored, shoved underground, or forbidden, our soul is starving—and there is a price to pay. Our heart grows weary. Our energy wanes. The sparkle in our eyes fades. We dry out. We lose our mojo. We become lost and uprooted. We feel restless, unhappy, confused, or angry. Depression and anxiety come visiting.

This inner turmoil we feel is our feminine instincts screaming for a return to our true self because deep inside we know we have lost something infinitely precious and beautiful. Our hopes and dreams are demanding our attention in their struggle to stay alive. But our conflict cannot be resolved until we release the fear, doubt, and worry that has such a tight grip on our lives.

Holy longings

Times of crisis and discontent in a woman's life are a call to return home to her true self. Whenever something inside us is lost in the dark, it eventually gives rise to mysterious longings. We become restless and irritable. We know deep down that something is missing but we have trouble articulating what we want. We sense something changing inside us. These feelings signal a need to return home to our true self.

When we are ready to return home to our true self, and reawaken our passion for life, we will stop turning away from our longings. We will stop ignoring the signs of trouble, stop running away, hesitating, making excuses, tricking ourselves, and saying everything is fine. Instead, we will find the courage to admit that everything is *not* fine and finally stand up for what is right and true for us. It takes fortitude to start caring for ourselves when we are used to caring for others. It takes courage to be emotionally honest, and it takes strength to make real changes in our life.

> *The longings from your soul are holy, and they come with a message: wake up, this is your life.*

The longings from your soul are holy, and they come with a message: wake up, this is *your* life; don't waste the precious gifts you have been given. Your soul is saying to you: I want to be who I really am. These longings we have are knocks at the door to our heart. They are saying to us, "Wake up! It's time to sing your song. and feel the bliss of being alive." As Rumi, the 13th-century Persian poet wrote, "When you do something from your soul, you feel a river moving in you, a joy." Holy longings show up to help us rediscover what it feels like to have river of joy flowing through us. They fill us with a raging desire to reclaim our rich, vibrant connection to Spirit.

We need to invite our longings, and not our fears, to the supper table, make friends with them, and give them nourishment. When we breathe life into our longings instead of fear, we turn toward what is summoning our soul, and away from what is heavy and lifeless. Perhaps you have no creative outlet, or time for self-care. Maybe you are in a toxic relationship, or have a hole in your life where something or someone once was. Whatever is going on, when you slow down and listen to your heart you will know what is missing, dead, or broken, and what needs to come alive so you can heal and feel whole again. Answering the call can feel dangerous, and we might be afraid of what may happen. But to turn away from our longings is to deny the sacred life force that flows through each one of us. We must not give fear the power to keep us in the shadows.

Often the bravest thing we can do is to simply start.

For a woman to truly love herself, she must welcome her longings and feed her passions. Regardless of how brave you are, the voice of fear may still arise. The voice of fear may tell you "Don't even bother trying," or, "who do you think you are?" It may say, "Hurry up, you need to get this done right now." The voice of fear may come from other people who, when we share our dreams with them, say to us, "Why would you want to do that?" Wherever the voice of fear comes from, we don't have to listen to it. We can start tending to the inner landscape of our soul where there are no limitations, only freedom. Often the bravest thing we can do is to simply start. We can follow our heart by taking one small step. We can choose to shape our life not out of fear of the unknown, but from the certainty of knowing that we are strong enough to face whatever comes our way.

My journey out of fear

As a young girl, I was quite independent and adventurous. Back then I raced my horse down dirt roads, and tromped through the woods by myself. But somehow, somewhere along the way of becoming a young woman, my true self went undercover. Despite my early years of being wild and free, fear and insecurity got a hold on me. I unconsciously internalized the gender stereotypes of what a young woman should look like and how a young woman should act. I began trying to fit the image of womanly perfection rather than loving and accepting who I was. At the time I was too afraid to ask myself: "Is this who I really want to be? Or is this what they expect me to be?"

Years later, married to my college sweetheart, and with two little children, I became restless. I was plagued by an endless litany of "shoulds" that didn't feel very fun anymore. It is getting late—I should be making supper. The house is a mess—I should be cleaning it. I wondered, "When did my life become one endless to-do list?" My desire to be everything to everyone was leading to heaps of guilt and self-judgment. Trying to find a healthy balance between the demands of outer necessity and the call of my inner life was pushing me into a crisis, one that I believe is part of every woman's journey. The question became: How can I take care of the ones I love while still nourishing my individual selfhood?

I entered a stage of searching. With stacks of books, I would disappear into the bathroom late at night after everyone was tucked into bed and fast asleep. Our big old claw-foot bathtub became my secret hide-away. While some people want to talk about their angst and their confusion, I simply wanted to be alone and read. An hour of soaking under a sea of bubbles expanded into infinity with a book in my hands. I inevitably emerged feeling like I had been talking with a good friend, one who understood me. Given the choice, I would have preferred to escape to a secluded tropical island where I could flop myself into a hammock and drink piña coladas all day. My problems would have disappeared— at least temporarily. But the truth was, that old bathtub worked wonderfully to soothe my soul. And so I kept asking questions, and doing the work of finding my way home.

My answers were not instantly helpful, but I was learning how to face my fears and listen to my heart. I finally had some realizations. My overwhelming love for my children had led me to the erroneous conclusion that I had to sacrifice myself on the altar of motherhood. All the "shoulds" and "buts" that I had internalized facilitated my self-sacrifice. I had adopted the belief that in order to be a good mother I had to set myself aside. Unconsciously, I had developed a superwoman complex, and I was withering from trying to be the perfect mother and wife. If someone had told me I was a perfectionist I would have denied it adamantly. Who, me? Never.

Through patient and gentle self-inquiry I was finally led to the answers I needed. I knew that in order to be the kind of woman I truly wanted to be—the kind that lives fearlessly without regrets—I had to take some of that mothering energy and give it to myself. My true self agreed, and miracles followed.

Releasing fear

Finding your way from fear to fearlessness does not depend on your social status, how much money you have, your education, or the state of your physical body. Every human being experiences fear. But fear doesn't have to determine your reality. Fearlessness grows when you say yes to the adventure of self-discovery. You move away from fear when you widen your vision for what is possible in your life. Courage takes hold when you look at the life you have been given, here and now, and decide to do the best you can with what you have. Fearlessness is less about predicting your future and more about becoming comfortable with the unknown. The antidote to fear is to humbly begin. Take one small step towards something that is calling your name.

Look at the life you have been given, here and now, and decide to do the best you can with what you have.

So how do you release fear? Start by challenging the idea that fear has any power over you. You can find your way there by listening to your longings and the dreams of your soul, and then bravely facing the shadows that surround them. This begins by quieting yourself, looking within, and asking sacred questions—questions that may scare you at first. Questions such as: What is holding me back from living my dreams? Am I living according to someone else's expectations or according to my true self? What am I running away from? What scares me the most? Entering into self-inquiry will ultimately lead to greater self-knowledge about the fears you may have. Once you face the fear that exists in different areas of your life, you can begin the work of dissolving them. You can turn the lock, release the fear, and open the door to your heart.

Releasing fear comes when we stop running away and look directly at it. When we bring our fears to the light of consciousness, they dissolve. When you are feeling heavy, dark, or tense, take a moment and just breathe. Instead of rushing around trying to be productive, stop, and face the feeling. Ask yourself: Right now, what am I afraid of? Is it a crushing weight of responsibility? The burden of being alone? Not having enough? Not being loved? Pain and suffering? Failure or disapproval? Not being perfect? Disappointing someone? Disappointing yourself?

The more you are willing to stand and face your fears, the more you can heal them. Hiding, running away and turning your back on your fears just allows them to grow. You can begin transforming your fear by acknowledging how you feel, and then taking a big cleansing breath into your body. Fear then becomes harmless energy rather than negative energy that holds you hostage. You can stop fear from affecting you by taking a moment to reflect on why you are feeling that way, and then give it love and release it.

The more you are willing to stand and face your fears, the more you can heal them.

Give yourself permission to let go of the pain and suffering that has occurred in your life because of fear. Create a picture in your mind where you put the lid firmly on top of the shoe box full of negativity. Stand on top of that shoe box and stomp the lid into place if you have to. Throw the box out the window. Then turn to the shoe box that is full of love and beauty and strength, all the good things that you know to be true. Fling the cover off and pull those feelings out of the box and put them on to wear. Imagine a pair of shoes that delight your soul. They feel wonderful, light, and magical—these shoes will take you everywhere, and anywhere you want to go.

Releasing fear also means we need to break free of negative self-talk, which can become a self-defeating addiction. If we are addicted to negativity, we must work hard to create new thoughts that are focused on higher states of well-being. If we are overwhelmed, or filled with doubt, we can take time right now to think about how far we have come and all we have achieved. We can learn to say, "I am worthy of good things in life!" It is vital that we learn how to feel good about ourselves and appreciate our life right now. When we do this, we can begin to have compassion for wherever we are at the moment. We can stop beating ourselves up because we are not perfect, and focus on the good that in our life, and in ourselves. A great way to start breaking free of negative self-talk is to look in the mirror each day and say, "I love you." No expectations, no judgment—just pure unconditional love and regard for yourself.

It is also important to let go of the negativity around you. Sometimes the doubt and fear we pick up from others prevents us from breathing life into our holy longings. As women, we are sensitive to what other people think and feel about us. We judge ourselves, second-guess ourselves, and withhold the love and acceptance that we deserve when we think other people don't like us. Ask yourself: Am I ready to let go of the expectations of others? Can I release the need to be perfect? How can I break free of the negativity that exists around me?

Finding your way from fear to fearlessness does not happen overnight. It takes patience, commitment, and hard work. It is an ongoing process that continues throughout your life. In each stage, you will be presented with new challenges that require a new kind of fearlessness. Keep asking yourself, "What would I do if I were not afraid?" If that becomes your mantra, you will grow in strength and courage. Your eyes will sparkle, and there will be a skip in your step because you feel confident, happy, and free. Standing tall and proud in your wisdom, beauty, and power, and making no apologies for who you are and who you are not—you will have indeed become a fearless woman.

You are meant to shine.

It is my hope that the rest of the questions in this book will help you find your way from fear to joy and freedom.

Julie Gohman, Ph.D.

What follows are some practices to help you build your courage muscles. Trust that you will find your way. Let Marianne Williamson's words inspire you as you walk to the edge and leap into the unknown, "Our deepest fear is not that we are inadequate. Our deepest fear is that we are powerful beyond measure. It is our light, not our darkness that most frightens us. We ask ourselves, Who am I to be brilliant, gorgeous, talented, and fabulous? Actually, who are you *not* to be?" You are meant to shine.

Tune Into Your Feminine Intuition

Learn how to distinguish between fear and intuition. Trustworthy intuitions will be more neutral, conveying information. You will feel it in your gut. Your intuition will never chip away at your self-worth or put you down; it is always there to serve you. Irrational fears, on the other hand, lack the gut-level feeling and clarity, and they are often highly emotional. Ask yourself if your fears are rooted in the past, or from trauma that you have experienced? Once you know where your fears are coming from, you can begin the process of releasing them. As your fears recede, you can begin trusting your feminine intuition more.

Invoke Feminine Energy

There are many ways you can bring the power of the divine feminine into your life. Perhaps you have a special angel or saint or Goddess that you connect with (mine is Mother Mary). Find a picture and place it somewhere special. Also consider the women who inspire you; they may be a dear friend, a loving grandmother, or a famous figure from history. Find photos of them, and let their presence lift you up, encourage you, and give you strength.

Breathe

We often hold our breath when we become anxious or fearful. Deep, slow breathing can have a profound affect on resetting the stress response. When we take a deep breath the vagus nerve is activated and that helps us relax. Try giving your complete attention to your in-breath and your out-breath. In this way, your body is united with your mind and you come home to yourself. Take a moment to honor how you are feeling. Recognize any tension or stress that exists in your body and let it go. Even one deep breath can make a difference. Better yet, try breathing in and out slowly five times, and observe how much better you feel.

Picture Your Ideal Life

The clearer you become about what you truly love and feel passionate about, the stronger your intention will become to create them in your life. Begin this exercise by closing your eyes and picturing your ideal life. Bring it alive and make it feel real—how do you feel? Where are you? Who are you with? What are you doing? Then make a list of the ten most important things from the ideal life that you imagined. How do they add joy, passion, and fulfillment to your life? Go through the list and listen to your heart to decide which things are most important. Look at this list on a regular basis to help you make decisions that move you in the direction of your dreams.

Julie Gohman, Ph.D.

Gratitude & Prayer

Start and end the day with gratitude for the strength, courage, and confidence that you are developing as a woman. Begin a regular practice of contemplative prayer or daily meditation. If you believe in angels, guides, a spiritual teacher, or that your grandmother is watching over you (I know mine is)—ask for their help to be fearless.

Create Action Steps

Think about your goals right now in life. Make a list. Ask yourself: If I could do anything, what would it be? Take ten minutes to translate your goals into action steps. What is one small thing you could do to bring you closer to your goals? Sometimes it might be obvious, and other times you will need to get creative to come up with your next step. Be bold, think in unlimited ways, and then commit to taking that first step. There is great power in beginnings.

Do One Thing Every Day That Scares You

Every day is an opportunity to perform small acts of bravery. Begin by thinking of what is outside your comfort zone. What are you reluctant to try? What are you avoiding? What terrifies you? If there is a shy, frightened little girl inside of you, why not help her climb out of her shell? Perhaps you are gathering the courage to try a new hairstyle, or say hello to someone you don't know. Sometimes you need to ask for help, or admit you made a mistake. If you are waiting to pitch a new idea at work, or request a raise, ask yourself what is the worst that could happen? Are you putting off a difficult conversation with someone close to you? Do it now before more time goes by and you have regrets. Do you think you are too old to go back to school? I met a woman in her eighties pursuing her doctorate. You are never too old to learn. Do you fear ending a relationship or losing a loved one? Maybe it is time to look honestly at the situation, painful as it may be, and take steps to change it. In all that you do try to become more daring.

Cultivate Your Inner Voice

Begin cultivating a strong inner voice that builds you up. Let your inner voice say things such as, "I can do this, I really can," or "I am confident and courageous." Plant "seed thoughts" in your mind that are kind and compassionate. Water those seeds and help them flourish so your inner voice becomes strong and clear. If you are surrounded by those who would keep you small, remember the words of Gertrude Stein who said, "Let me listen to me and not to them."

Fear can be a complex feeling that keeps us from experiencing life as we would like it to be. But every day we can find the courage to face our fears—the little ones and the big ones. We can release them when we are ready, and begin living from a secure and powerful place within ourselves. Remember, fear is a feeling, not a fact of life.

The question to ask yourself is:
What would I do if I were not afraid?

Julie Gohman, Ph.D.

For Joy and Freedom

*May every restless wind and wave of confusion
find a shore of stillness in your heart.*

*May the whispers of longing
find a place at your table.*

*May your inner voice become a beacon
graced with strength and courage.*

*May you welcome every shape of desire
that yearns to be born.*

*May you be blessed as you make the journey
from fear to joy and freedom.*

The First Sacred Question

What would I do if I were not afraid?

What would I do if I were not afraid?

The Second Sacred Question

What is My Soul Story?

*Everywoman has the leading role
in her own unfolding life story.*
—Jean Shinoda Bolen

In Greek mythology, there is a story about the Goddesses Demeter and Persephone. It is a story so important that it became the basis for the Eleusinian Mysteries, the most sacred religious rituals in ancient Greece for over two thousand years. As the story goes, the young and carefree Persephone was gathering flowers in a meadow and playing with friends. When she reached for a particularly beautiful flower, a narcissus, the ground suddenly opened beneath her. A gold chariot pulled by black horses came from the deep—with Hades inside it. He grabbed Persephone and swiftly plunged back into the abyss. Persephone screamed for help from Zeus, the king of the gods on Mount Olympus, but none came.

Demeter, Persephone's mother, heard the echoes of her screams and rushed out to find her. Demeter searched for her daughter for nine days and nights without stopping to eat, sleep or rest. Demeter was filled with outrage and grief after finding out from Helios, the God of the Sun, that Hades had kidnapped her daughter to be his bride. She left Mount Olympus and wandered aimlessly through the countryside, covering her radiant beauty with the disguise of an old woman. Because she was the Goddess of Grain, nothing could grow, and nothing could be born. Famine threatened to destroy the human race. Zeus and all the other Gods begged Demeter to restore fertility to the land. But Demeter said she would not allow anything to grow until her daughter was safely returned to her. Finally, Zeus sent Hermes, the Messenger, to Hades and commanded the return of Persephone. With great joy, mother and daughter were reunited, and Demeter restored fertility to the earth.

The story of Demeter and Persephone, in many ways, is the everlasting story of womanhood. Persephone represents the young girl we once were. She doesn't know who she wants to be and is often waiting for someone or something to transform her life. Persephone is the part of us that wants to please other people. She represents the way women have been conditioned to be passive, compliant, and charming. Persephone is the child-woman who is not yet aware of her beauty or strength and hasn't yet developed confidence in herself. Over time, however, Persephone grows up and comes into her own, becoming the Queen of the Underworld.

Demeter represents the maternal instinct in women to provide nourishment to others. She is the mother archetype who provides food and spiritual sustenance. As mothers, most of us relate to Demeter because we too would do whatever it takes to keep our children safe and well. The mother archetype may show up in women as the desire to have a baby, but it also is lived through relationships where women are naturally generous and caring to others. Women who go into the helping professions, and become teachers, nurses, and counselors, for example, often have a great need to nurture others. When a woman becomes a mother, it is one of the most powerful and life-changing events that shapes the future of her soul story.

Your soul story

Close your eyes. In your mind picture a rose; it can be any color—soft pink, velvety red, bright yellow, crisp white. Imagine the rose as a small bud, fresh with the morning dew. Then, ever so slowly, see the rose as it begins opening. Pay attention to the shape of the petals, the subtle variations of color, the fragrance. Bring the picture alive. Watch as petal by petal the whole flower unfolds slowly. Illuminate the vision in your mind until the rose captures all your senses. Hold it gently for it is precious. The rose is you, and each luscious petal represents a chapter in your soul story.

Have you ever thought about your journey through life as a soul story? Although we enjoy reading stories and watching them unfold on the big screen, we seldom consider that we are the stars of our own story and it's playing on the big screen called life. Marion Woodman, a Jungian analyst and prolific writer about feminine psychology, wrote that a "soul story" is one with roots of understanding that dig deep into our hearts. It is where our head and heart join to find the inner truth that sets us free.

Our life is a story and we are all storytellers. There are many stories being told simultaneously: the story that we are living right now, the story from our past, and the story waiting for us down the road. Our development as women is intrinsically connected to the stories we are telling. We keep writing, revising, and weaving together the elements of our story according to how we see life at any given moment.

Our life is a story and we are all storytellers.

It is an act of devotion to your true self to allow your story to emerge. As your story begins to take shape, the roots of understanding will take hold in your heart. Patterns and symbols will appear. More than piecemeal facts, or disconnected fragments over time—your story will represent the evolution of your soul. You will come to see how you have been creating your "soul story" every day of your life.

To allow our stories to unfold gracefully, we need to allow them to move with their own momentum. This is how we discern our truth from our fiction. Does it feel natural or is it forced? Does it have its own rhythm or are we pushing it along? Our story may change depending on the day and the hour, but will always retain the essence of who we are. That is why we must stay in close touch with the stories we are weaving—they represent our inner life, and what it means to be a woman. They form a vision where our memories from the past and our dreams for the future come together to knit the meaning of our life.

Finding Your Story

Finding your soul story will require you to drop from your head into your heart. Not only will you be delving into the real events of your life, you will also be exploring the emotions that surround them. Your soul will need to lead the way as your journey is told.

We are all telling stories whether we realize it or not. We are giving voice to what we believe about ourselves every day. Our most fundamental assumptions we have about life are so basic to our thinking and feeling that we don't even realize they govern the way we create our reality. There are an infinite number of core beliefs that we may have, but there are six common patterns that negatively affect us, according to Shakti Gawain, author of *Creative Visualization*. Number one—*I am powerless. I'm not responsible for what happens to me.* Number two—*There's not enough (money, love, time, energy, jobs, space, etc.) to go around.* Number three—*Life is a struggle. Things are hard, but that's okay because I'll get my reward when I die.* Number four—*I'm not worthy. I don't deserve love or happiness or prosperity.* Number five—*I'm afraid to take risks. What if I fail, or worse yet, what if I'm successful?* Number six—*I don't trust myself, or the universe. What if my feelings or intuitions are wrong?* If any of these beliefs are limiting you, ask yourself if you are ready to let them go and begin affirming a new story. A story where you are powerful, prosperous, and worthy of every good thing. A story where life is not a constant struggle. A story where you do not live in fear but trust your feelings and intuitions to lead you to a joyful and satisfying life.

Our challenges can be a source of great inspiration—celebrating where we have overcome something difficult in our life. However, if we get stuck in the negative aspects of our stories, we are stripped of our personal power. Apathy takes hold, and we begin sounding like a broken record of why we can't be happy or successful. Talking about our problems instead of our joys can become an addiction that leaves us feeling powerless over our own life. Instead, begin affirming the highest and best for yourself—and watch as your world begins transforming.

Begin affirming the highest and best for yourself.

Past the challenges are the choices you make in your life. If you are focusing on the choices you have made, your story goes from apathy to empowerment. You recognize that you are a choice maker and that you have made the path that has brought you to this point in time. When you honestly examine your choices, you begin to dig deeper into self-inquiry. You are confronted with important questions. Why did you make the choices you have made? How did it feel? Did you listen to your intuition? Were you trying to please someone? What were the consequences to you personally? Our choices reveal our state of consciousness. We can examine our choices and learn from them, not with judgment or criticism, but with acceptance and compassion. We are doing the very best we know how. Dwelling on choices helps us see that our story is constantly changing according to how powerful we feel in our lives.

Our choices reveal our state of consciousness.

Choices are always followed by consequences. These are the outcomes that we face as a result of our choices and the choices of others. Good storytelling is never complete without knowing what happened in the end. The outcomes help us celebrate our achievements, as well as forgive the parts of our story that need healing. Sometimes things happen in our life that we are ashamed of, things we would rather forget. Rarely does life go exactly as planned. However, it is as Brené Brown writes, "Loving ourselves through the process of owning our story is the bravest thing we'll ever do." Owning our story means we stop running away from the painful experiences. Every woman has tasted the sweetness of love, the fear of loss, the pain of heartache. We wouldn't be who we are without them. By giving voice to all of these experiences, we can understand ourselves better. We can acknowledge that everything we have been through has taught us something important about ourselves. Ultimately, we are not what has happened to us in the past; we are what we choose to become today.

The Spiral In Every Woman's Story

My research exploring women's lives surprised me. As I interviewed the women in my study, most of them told me they had never slowed down enough to think about their personal story of womanhood. I asked them questions about their personal development, motherhood, spirituality, and the joys and struggles they have experienced along the way. Most of the women got teary-eyed as they reflected on their life. I had to stop frequently during the interview process as waves of emotion would roll in unexpectedly. I believe it was the power of telling their story and having someone listen deeply and completely that made the interviews so cathartic for the women in my study.

What I discovered through my data analysis is that every woman has themes spiraling through her story. For example, one participant, Tara told about leaving home as a teenager to escape her abusive mother. Then, as a young single mother, she found herself in an abusive relationship to a man whom she later married. She eventually found the courage to leave him too. Now, in her 50's, she is a passionate advocate for women and works to help others who are in abusive situations. The spirals in Tara's story revolve around being courageous, standing up for herself, and honoring her worthiness for respect and love. The journey for her, like most women, was not a straight path. She did not move directly from being oppressed to being free. There were dips, lulls, and periods of confusion and darkness along the way. Intuitively Tara knew what she had to do but getting there wasn't easy. In *Pathways of the Soul*, Hillevi Ruumet, Ph.D. writes, "We wander in what ultimately feels like a spiral with an unobstructed path leading us through, but in the walking it seems more like a convoluted maze. We see our path clearly only in hindsight." Oftentimes, we look back, and we know we did what we were meant to do; there is a sense of destiny, or purpose.

As you begin contemplating your soul story, you will discover the spirals that swirl through your life. Within the spirals exist the past, the present, and the future. Our perceptions of our past and our vision of the future are influenced by where we are right now. Your story will change depending on your focus of attention. When you change part of your story, you change your reality. For example, if you tell your soul story from a position of powerlessness, your reality is that you are a victim of your life. But if you tell the same story from a position of choice and responsibility, your reality becomes one that is infused with courage and determination.

Part of finding our story is getting lost.

Part of finding our story is getting lost. When we are lost, we begin opening up and listening to our soul because we feel vulnerable and are filled with so many unanswered questions. Sometimes when we are in transition, or in a period of chaos, where we have lost our way, we discover it is exactly what we need in order to find our path again. Sometimes we must break down in order to break through. As we turn inward and listen, we discover a deeper truth. Our true self is at the center of our soul story, and yet our true self goes beyond our story and is eternal. Knowing this allows us to hold our stories lightly, and release them when it is time.

Sharing your story with a trusted friend or group of women is one way to get feedback. Sometimes when we are too close to the story, it becomes difficult, if not impossible, to step back and be a witness. Caution is advised however if you decide to share your story with others. Many women find they have an unconscious desire to please other people with their story. Remember—this is *your* soul story, so share it with people you trust. Your memories and perceptions might not match what other people remember about the past. Let it go. Stay strong and honor your own spiritual journey.

Sharing Our Soul Stories

In a sense, your story is uniquely your own, yet still part of the collective whole that taps into ancient feminine roots. Our lives may differ in the details, but ultimately, our feminine nature joins us together in ways that elude men. When we find common ground with our sisters in this world, we honor the feminine and deepen our connections to one another. Women's stories are soul food—they heal us, nourish us, and make us whole. And when they are told from a deep place of truth, from a place of soulfulness, they become a powerful source of light for the world. As the Native Americans taught, stories are a form of medicine that bring us back to the truth of who we are.

For women, there is often a deep resonance between their personal story and the stories of other women. Many women experience an intuitive recognition when there is a match between their inner feelings and desires and the outer picturing of women's lives. There is a heartfelt connection when we see and hear what other women go through. Our stories come together. A voice inside of us says, "Yes, I have felt that way too. I've been there. I understand." Soul stories allow us to express our joys and struggles as women as real lived experience, nothing fancy, nothing hidden, nothing to be ashamed of.

> *Women's stories are soul food—they heal*
> *us, nourish us, and make us whole.*

When we have the courage to share our stories, we grow in self-awareness, self-acceptance, and self-love. We see that our struggles and disappointments are not just our own; many other women have gone through the same things. We are not alone. In a sense, our stories are universal. By opening our hearts and truly hearing one another, we create a community for celebrating womanhood. Our stories become a vehicle for healing and transformation—they bring meaning, hope, and vision together.

There are many practices that can help jumpstart the process of discovering your soul story. I have listed a few that are powerful, creative, and inspiring. These practices (journaling, marking *descansos* on your timeline, writing a memoir, singing, dancing, and painting your story) will help you articulate your spiritual journey as a woman. Find a practice that appeals to you and enjoy the process as your story comes to life. Best of all, there are no deadlines and no rules for how you must do it!

Begin Journaling

Journaling is an ongoing process of seeing, naming and understanding yourself and your experiences. There is never an end product with keeping a journal; it is always a work in progress. Find a journal (also known as a diary or notebook) that you find beautiful, and use a pen that feels good in your hand. My journal has a bright red oriental flower on the front and a quote by Rumi on the flap that says, "We have fallen into the place where everything is music." I like to use brightly colored pens and I occasionally glue pictures in my journal as well. When I open it up to write, it feels like a secret hiding place. An alternative that is growing in popularity is keeping an e-journal on your computer. (For a lovely e-journal to accompany this book, please visit my website www.juliegohman.com and download it for free.) There is a certain pleasure that comes when you have a place that is all your own to express the things you wouldn't dare say out loud.

Your journal can become a sacred home where all the ambiguities of life can be expressed. Here you can rant, waffle, question, and dream. This is where all the secret places inside of you are welcome. You can collect ideas, play around with words, and discover new insights. Your journal becomes the place where you can put down all the words that get stuck in your throat, a common problem for many women. Your frozen tears can stream down the pages. The shadow side of your psyche, and those things you have buried deep in your unconscious can emerge safely for the first time.

Creating a daily ritual of journaling is a lovely gift to give yourself. Some women find great pleasure in curling up in bed with a hot cup of tea and their journal before going to sleep at night. Quiet time for self-reflection at the end of the day often prompts a rich dream life during the night, another powerful source of information about our soul story. Some women enjoy a morning ritual for journal

Julie Gohman, Ph.D.

writing, with the intention to start the day connected to their deeper impulses. You could incorporate your dreams from the night before into your journal pages. However you do it, try to find a time and a place where you can relax and be undisturbed. Keep it private. Lock it away or hide it. Your journal is for your eyes only. Treasure the freedom to say whatever you want. Let the pages reveal your wonder and joy as well as your pain and sorrow. Take time to reflect on what you have written. Looking back through your journal pages will help you discover the themes that are spiraling through your story. Your journal will become where you can begin reclaiming your true self. It can be as author Virginia Woolf once said about her diary: a place to bring order to the chaos in your life.

Creating a daily ritual of journaling is a lovely gift to give yourself.

Make a Timeline and Mark Your Descansos

In *Women Who Run With the Wolves*, Clarissa Pinkola Estés introduced the concept of "*descansos.*" In Mexico and the Southwest US descansos are the "resting places" where people have died—from a car accident, or when a pedestrian was killed—marked by small white crosses and shrines. These memorials mark the exact spot where people's dreams and lives suddenly came to an end. Symbolically, *descansos* mark a death. Applied to our own life, they allow us to think about where our dreams, aspirations, and hopes have died.

Every woman's life is marked by literal and figurative deaths. People we love die, hopes and dreams are lost, tragedy strikes, illness comes unexpectedly, and loved ones disappoint or leave us. These events change our lives and the lives of those around us in ways that we never anticipated. The journey of womanhood is filled with experiences, some that bring new life and light, and some that bring darkness and death—we continually fluctuate between brokenness and wholeness. No one escapes unchanged.

Most of us want to turn away from the suffering that death causes, and we go to great lengths to avoid it. But the more we stuff our feelings, the deeper they go. Eventually, we may experience what the mystics call "the dark night of the soul," a period of deep despair, loss and grief. During these bleak periods in our life, we are called to find the courage to deal with the unfinished business from our past. When we do so, we emerge stronger and more empowered in our lives. Our suffering becomes a catalyst for a great transformation.

When we create a timeline and mark our *descansos* we mourn the loss when someone we loved died, or a dream was lost, or part of our life faded away. Estés writes, "Women have died a thousand deaths before they are twenty years old....To make *descansos* means taking a look at your life and marking where the small deaths, *las muertes chicitas*, and the big deaths, *las muertes grandotas*, have taken place."

Creating a timeline that reveals all our sorrows can be a transformative practice —it helps us to feel and to heal. It requires that we acknowledge all our suffering with love and compassion for ourselves. Along with love and compassion, we also offer forgiveness to ourselves, and to others. We must be gentle. *Descansos* mark the dark times and bittersweet moments of life. They are love notes to our suffering. They lead to our liberation from the past, and allow us to start with a clean page ready for a new story.

When we mark our timeline with *descansos* we are putting our pain to rest—we are giving it a resting place outside of us, just like the white crosses we see by the side of the road. We are honoring the losses we have suffered so that we may finally put our painful experiences behind us. We no longer have to blame ourselves for things in the past. We can let go and break free from the limiting beliefs and patterns that are holding us back.

What are you ready to let go of?

When I made my timeline and marked my *descansos*, I used a long piece of butcher paper and some markers. I drew a line and marked my birth at one end. Then I closed my eyes, relaxed my body, and went back to my earliest memories. Most of my early memories were quite happy. I was a free-spirited child who loved to run and play outside in the woods and swim in the lakes—and I was fortunate to have parents who let me. Then a pit formed in my stomach and heaviness filled my heart. The biggest death in my childhood happened when I was seven. My parents divorced, and everything in my life suddenly changed. In my mind, I had come to terms with my parents' divorce many years ago, but there was still a massive ball of confusion, pain, and grief in my heart. I still felt deep sorrow for what I had lost as a child.

Tears slid down my cheeks as I looked at the big cross I had drawn on my timeline. Even though the timeline was straight, I knew that the insecurity and fear I felt as a little girl was still circling around in my life. I listened for what longed to be healed in me. I listened to the rhythm of my heartbeat. I knew that it was time to forgive my parents and let go of the pain from my childhood.

Ask yourself what you are ready to let go of? It may be something from many years ago, or it may be something that happened yesterday. Creating your timeline and marking your *descansos* may bring tears as your heart opens up to old memories. It is like taking a key that is being offered to you so you may let yourself out of the prison of the past. Catherine Ponder wrote, "So many people miss their present blessings because they are still lamenting unhappy experiences of the past." Peace comes to us when we see life as the painful yet beautiful journey that it is. When you have mourned the past, and marked every *descansos* on your timeline, you can look to the future with an open heart — you have awakened to the precious now.

Write a Memoir

Alice Walker once said, "There's an ecstatic side to writing. It's like jazz. It just has a life." Writing a memoir may seem like a crazy idea at first, but it's not. By putting into words what you have experienced you create a vehicle for growth and transformation. For many women, writing a memoir is a deeply healing process and an act of empowerment.

What is a memoir? It is a collection of memories about the moments in your life that make you who you are. A memoir could be two pages or two hundred pages. It could be about one day in your life or a particular stage that you went through that was poignant and meaningful. Writing a memoir is a way to help you make sense of your life. The goal is to eventually get down to the truth. A memoir requires that you dig deep, and go to those uncomfortable places inside yourself. It also requires that you create space in your life to hear the whispers from your soul. It is as much about listening to the stories that are inside you as it is about writing them down on paper.

According to Linda Myers, author of *The Power of Memoir*, there are many reasons to write a memoir. One of the main reasons is that through memoir you gain a deeper understanding of yourself and your life. Many writers find the process also creates a newfound sense of hope for the future. You may want to write a memoir to create a legacy for your family. Think of all the wonderful stories that you want your family and friends to remember. Another reason could be to expose an injustice or settle an emotional score (anger, revenge, acceptance, forgiveness). You may find that writing a memoir is a way to explore controversial issues that are difficult to talk about. You can also share your unique experiences in the world. Subjects such as travel adventures, illness and recovery, important relationships, and spiritual quests can come to life in the pages of your memoir.

Dig deep, and go to those uncomfortable places inside yourself.

My colleague and mentor, Diana Raab, Ph.D., is a poet and memoirist. Her book, *Healing with Words: A Writer's Cancer Journey* describes what she went through when she was diagnosed with breast cancer, and then five years later multiple myeloma. Her story is raw, honest, tender, and sometimes painful. She wrote, "There are a number of messages I have taken from the cancer journey, but for me, the most important one is that the diagnosis of cancer should be considered a turning point that sets you free to fulfill or examine dreams that can no longer wait. It can be a time when you feel infinite strength and are prompted to look inside yourselves not only for ways to cope, but for secrets to your happiness. It is about understanding what you really want in life. Many times this means reaching back into your childhood to examine what your passions were back then. Some of your secrets may lie in those years. My family and friends always encouraged my writing because they understood its healing powers. In a profound way, having cancer brought out the poet in me, which has been dormant since my youth. For this I am so thankful." Diana has since become an award-winning author of eight books and has written hundreds of poems and articles. She has taken her experiences with cancer and used them to become an advocate of writing as a vehicle for healing, transformation, and empowerment. She now teaches classes and facilitates workshops to help others unlock their personal stories. As she wrote in her memoir, "Write on! It's for you. It's for your health. It's for your life!"

Sing It, Dance It, Paint It

For those of you who don't enjoy writing, or feel as if the right words don't come easily to you, there are other ways you can tell your soul story. The creative arts are a wonderful area to explore if you want to find a way to express your story that is more your style. It is not essential to write your story in words. If you enjoy singing, you may find that giving voice to your experiences through song is the most healing path for you. Ask yourself: If there was a song that came from my soul what would it be? Finding your passion is the key to unlocking the best way to express your story. If you are a dancer, then moving your body can become an exquisite form of storytelling. No words needed. Your movements will speak for you. The art of dance is a powerful avenue for creative expression and transformation. Perhaps you are a painter at heart. Your soul story may emerge best when you have a paintbrush in your hand and a blank canvas in front of you.

There is an endless array of options when it comes to the creative arts. You may want to try sculpture, or pottery. Another way that many women tell stories is through pictures. Instead of making scrapbooks for your children, how about making one for yourself? Creating visual collages, much like a vision board that plots your hopes and dreams, is another way to express your story. Gather pictures, use markers, glue, and favorite quotes to make a unique picture board that represents your life. You don't have to be an artist to make a collage, and it can be a fun activity to do with others. There is no limit to how you can use your energy and imagination to express your soul story.

The question to ask yourself is: What is my soul story?

For Your Soul Story

*May you find the courage
to free your voice
as you encounter
the shadows of the past
and the whispers of your soul.*

*May you learn to hold them
tenderly yet honestly
remembering the stories
from yesterday
waiting to be told.*

*May you be blessed
with an open heart
and a creative spirit
that you may discover
the beauty of who you are.*

*May you find your story
the endings and beginnings
the joys and sorrows
and may it begin to heal you
petal by luscious petal.*

Julie Gohman, Ph.D.

What is my soul story?

The Second Sacred Question

What is my soul story?

The Third Sacred Question

Am I Ready For Wabi Sabi Love?

*There is an instinctive seeking of all things for love.
Love is another name for life.*
—Emma Curtis Hopkins

Love is a fundamental human need. Babies die when they are deprived of love and affection. Children thrive when they are surrounded with it, and adults wither when it's missing from their lives. We need to give love, and we need to be loved. Our need for affection and togetherness is a powerful motivator that is at the root of most everything we do. As women, we find meaning and purpose in our lives through our loving connections to others. In fact, in no small way, whom we know and love has much to do with who we become. The web of relationships that we find ourselves in is intrinsically tied to how we see ourselves, how we love, how we grow and change, and how we weather the storms of life.

Love is a timeless subject that never fails to enthrall us. Love has been on our minds and in our hearts since the beginning of time, and no story is ever complete without it.

Perhaps now, more than any other time in history, we want to know how to create and nurture lasting love. We want to know what it takes to make love grow, and we want to know how to avoid the mistakes, so we never lose the love that we have.

Despite the worrisome statistics about divorce today, most of us still have hope for finding love and keeping it alive. Our eternal belief in love probably began when we were little girls, from fairy tales like Sleeping Beauty and Cinderella. We were led to believe that falling in love meant riding off into the sunset with Prince Charming, happily ever after. While fairy-tale thinking can be magical fun, too much of it leaves us believing that we must find that someone special to ride off into the sunset with in order to be whole and complete. Whether we realize it or not, we have been conditioned to expect a fantasy. No wonder we find ourselves disappointed, dissatisfied, and disillusioned with our relationships when they do not live up to the fantasy in our minds. Our Prince Charming begins looking like a frog real fast as we juggle the day-to-day responsibilities of children, careers, and home—and there is no magic wand or glass slipper to help us out or carry us away.

A loving partnership is one in which you are always free to be yourself.

We can shift our thinking by realizing that romantic love is less about the fantasy of happily ever after, and more about the wonder of two souls meeting and choosing to continue the journey of life together. Love and togetherness are less about finding the "perfect soul mate" and more about discovering who you are so you can honestly share your true self with another. A loving partnership is one in which you are always free to be yourself. Love is a mystical experience, a dance of give and take, a home for your soul where there is respect and dignity. When we commit our love to another, we are saying, "Come into my life, let us grow and struggle and wonder together along this beautiful yet imperfect path we are traveling."

Love is the language of the soul.

To share our life with another person, day in and day out, with all our little quirks, annoying habits, and idiosyncrasies is no small feat. Despite all of the challenges, most of us continue to treasure our relationships—because without love the color fades from our life. As Christian mystic, St. Theresa of Avila, wrote, "It is love alone that gives worth to all things." Love is the language of the soul.

In W*abi Sabi Love: The Ancient Art of Finding Perfect Love in Imperfect Relationships*, Arielle Ford shares how the concept of wabi sabi helped her stop striving for perfection. She became a "Wabi Sabi artisan" and applied the principles to her love life. Ford explains wabi sabi love: "It is the art of loving your partner's imperfections rather than indulging in the fantasy that your relationship can fire on all cylinders only when both people are acting perfectly and behaving in ways that are acceptable to the other."

If we want to change our perceptions about love, and improve our relationships, including the one we have with ourselves, we can look to wabi sabi for guidance. Wabi sabi has its roots in Japanese Zen philosophy. There are three main principles of wabi sabi—nothing lasts forever, nothing is perfect, and nothing is ever finished. The wisdom that is found in this philosophy is based on humility, simplicity, and acceptance of both the joys and sorrows of life. Wabi sabi, in its essence, helps us to relax, stay centered, and live from our heart and soul. It is timeless, simple, and enduring. Wabi sabi asks us to see the naked beauty of life as it is.

Wabi sabi love means we practice loving ourselves and our partner, imperfections and all. It does not, however, mean we accept unhealthy situations, or deny our right to make changes when they are needed. It is about looking at our partner and ourselves, and focusing on what is right instead of focusing on what is wrong. Practicing wabi sabi love helps us to embrace the gifts of imperfection so that we can live and love with our eyes wide open.

The wisdom of wabi sabi teaches that real love begins inside.

Whether we have a partner or would like to find one, the wisdom of wabi sabi teaches that real love begins inside us. Releasing ourselves from the constant striving for perfection frees us. Accepting impermanence allows us to appreciate everything all the more here and now. Approaching people with modesty and humility encourages them to open up to us. We can then form strong and lasting connections that are not ego-driven or hierarchal, but based on equality, respect, and kindness.

A deep commitment to loving and respecting ourselves in all our imperfection is one of the greatest works of wabi sabi. By accepting who we are, we can then accept others just as they are. Ultimately, we can open our mind and heart to the imperfect beauty that exists everywhere in the world.

Loving yourself

To love others, you must first love yourself. You cannot give to others what you do not have for yourself—this is especially true of love. You cannot be to others what you are not to yourself. If you respect yourself, you will show respect to others. If you can forgive yourself when you make mistakes, you will find it easier to forgive others too. Only to the depth and extent that you love yourself can you love others. How we love others is always a reflection of how we love ourselves.

Loving yourself does not mean that you are like the evil witch in *Snow White* who constantly looks in the mirror at her own reflection. Self-love is not self-indulgence or self-pity. Loving yourself means you fundamentally care for and respect who you are, and make choices that support your long-term health and well-being. Loving yourself is about genuinely appreciating your own presence. You do not feel the need to be the same as everyone else, but rather you delight in discovering your uniqueness and sharing it with others. When you truly love yourself, you continue to explore all the fantastic possibilities that lie dormant within you, knowing it is never too late to transform who you are. You believe in your own infinite potential.

> *Offer yourself kindness and understanding instead of criticism and judgment.*

Loving yourself means you recognize your innate goodness. When you are having a difficult time, you offer yourself compassion. You stop, acknowledge your pain, and ask, How can I care for myself right now? What would be uplifting to my soul in this moment? When you experience personal failings, you offer yourself kindness and understanding instead of criticism and judgment. According to Kristin Neff, Ph.D., author of *Self-Compassion*, having compassion for yourself means that you honor and accept your humanness. Life will bring frustrations, losses, limitations, and disappointments, but when you open your heart to your experiences instead of fighting against them, you will feel more compassion for yourself. Nothing is wasted if you use it wisely. You can learn from everything that happens to you.

How can we practice loving ourselves? We can use the principles of wabi sabi and begin embracing our imperfections. We can learn to see the beauty in them. When we find ourselves getting angry when life does not go the way we want, we can acknowledge our pain and suffering and offer ourselves sympathy and kindness. When we are warm and gentle to ourselves, we are more likely to feel hope instead of despair.

Loving ourselves also means recognizing our shared human experience. To be human is to be mortal. We are vulnerable beings. Therefore, when we love ourselves we acknowledge that who we are has been affected by factors outside our control. We live in an intricate web of relationships, what Buddhist teacher Thich Nhat Hahn calls "interbeing." We are influenced by everything around us. When we acknowledge our interdependence, we can stop taking everything so personally. We can remember that we are part of a greater whole. In Africa, there is a philosophy called "Ubuntu." Ubuntu essentially means that our humanity is intertwined with one another. We are only human, and what we are going through is part of the human experience.

We are part of a greater whole.

Learning how to welcome all your emotions, both positive and negative is also part of loving yourself. Observe the waves of emotion that flow through you with mindful awareness. In other words, try to receive them in a non-judgmental way without denying or suppressing them. Do not ignore your pain—instead, listen to what it is trying to tell you. For example, when you are tired, give yourself permission to rest. If you are feeling frustrated with your work, consider a career change or take steps to improve your current situation. If you feel miserable in a relationship, seek help to make it better, or consider the possibility (as difficult and scary as it may be) of ending it and moving on. When you love yourself, you make changes that respect and honor who you are and what you need to be happy, because you are worth it. Self-love allows you to develop a larger perspective about how to embrace all your emotions instead of getting swept away by them. When you have a loving relationship with yourself, you have found a priceless treasure that no one can ever take away.

Embracing imperfection

When we genuinely acknowledge that we are not perfect, we can surrender our constant urge to judge and criticize ourselves, and others. There is no place in life for expecting perfection from anyone. We can stop wishing for the perfect life, the perfect relationship, the perfect body, the perfect job, the perfect house, the perfect vacation, or the perfect family. This does not mean we become complacent or that we put up with toxic or abusive situations. Indeed, we never stop growing or striving to make our life better. The nature of life is constant change. But we no longer need to criticize ourselves when, inevitably, we stumble or make a mistake, because we have not failed in any way. Instead, we can consciously forgive ourselves and embrace our experiences. Sometimes our soul evolves much more quickly when we stumble and fall than when we are doing everything "right."

If our partnership is in turmoil, it is easy to become disheartened. Every relationship has its moments of sadness, disappointment, and frustration. The important thing to remember is that it is how you choose to deal with these emotions that makes the difference. Wabi sabi teaches us to approach problems with tenderness and in calm, quiet ways. We need to practice being good to ourselves and to each other, especially during difficult times. Sometimes it is in the small gestures we offer to each other—a kind word, an understanding smile, a soft touch—that shows our compassion and devotion. We must ask ourselves: Will I turn away when life gets hard, or will I become a helpmate? Can I dwell in appreciation instead of judgment? Can I set aside my righteousness? Am I attaching strings to my love? Can I allow more freedom in my relationships?

We need to practice being good to ourselves and to each other.

The more we accept and appreciate who we are—with all of our unique flaws and quirks—the more we can live in harmony with our partner and loved ones, despite their flaws and quirks (as long as those flaws and quirks are not harmful to us). When we release our partner from the demand for perfection, we can approach our relationship with the kindness and understanding it deserves. The less we try to fix and control and demand things, the happier the relationship will be. We can give our partner the dignity and respect that we desire for ourselves.

Imperfection does not preclude beauty, and in reality, imperfections often enhance beauty. Whether it is a crack in a beautiful vase or the trunk of a tree, fallen petals in an otherwise perfect garden, a bump on the nose, a scar on a body, a crooked tooth or wrinkles on a face, all these "imperfections" are part of a beautiful whole. As the French say, imperfections add a certain *je ne sais quoi*—"I do not know what"—to a person, place, or thing, that can, in fact, increase their beauty. The *je ne sais quoi* is perhaps a connection to the mysterious pull we feel towards the beauty that is in all things just as they are.

Learning to accept, and even appreciate, the imperfections and the beauty in our partner enables us to value and focus on what is truly important—our love. When we get caught up in the trivial things that are ultimately insignificant, we miss the opportunity to connect with our partner at the heart level, the place inside us that hungers for closeness. Often we get upset not because of what is happening around us, but because of what is happening inside us. Our expectations of how things are *supposed* to be create disharmony within us. It is here that wabi sabi teaches us to let go of our preconceived notions and let life be the imperfect mess that it is.

Look within to discover what is really bothering you.

In every relationship, there will be times of hardship. Relationship experts claim that all marriages, even the great ones, have irreconcilable differences. Sometimes they are deal-breakers, but often they are issues that can be dealt with by cultivating the qualities of deep listening, non-judgment, mutual respect and appreciation, emotional honesty, and personal responsibility. If your partner is disrespectful, derogatory, abusive, or harms you in any way – that is a deal-breaker. You deserve to be treated better. But if your relationship is rooted in respect and equality, and yet you find that you are struggling with your differences, consider how your situation has the potential to be transformed. Instead of assigning blame and trying to change your partner, look within to discover what is really bothering you.

Transforming habitual patterns that exist in our relationships is difficult. We often feel sad, angry, guilty, and stuck when we repeat the same defeating behaviors over and over. And the longer we've been together, the more entrenched these patterns usually are. The good news is that underneath old patterns is something begging us to "wake up." If we are willing to persevere, and be patient, we can see how our relational difficulties are actually opportunities for our own awakening, and for our relationship to become stronger and more stable. It takes courage to examine our habitual patterns and to begin changing them. The first step is to become self-aware. Notice how your body feels when you act out of habit. Explore alternate ways you can react, communicate, and work with your relationship issues. Consider the power of the choices you make everyday. Ask yourself if you are acting in ways that feel right to you.

If we want our relationships to grow and flourish, we must be committed. Without commitment we cannot truly see the beautiful soul of another. When we are committed to our partner, trust becomes the foundation for growing together. Emotional honesty and vulnerability pave the way for a love that has no secrets. A love like this begins with a choice, an intention that reflects a pure desire for spiritual partnership with another human being. Spiritual partnership is based on the idea that we come together not to live happily ever after, but to help each other grow spiritually, as equals, as individuals, surrounded with the energy of compassion, generosity, and openness.

What do I want to create in this relationship?

If we don't like the relationship we have with our partner, we can make the conscious intention to change it. We need to ask ourselves, "What do I want to create in this relationship?" If part of us wants to make it better, and part of us wants to end it, we will become splintered. These conflicting intentions will cause us to struggle, feel restless, and experience much turbulence in our relationships. In the end, whatever intention is stronger, whether conscious or unconscious, will ultimately determine what happens. If we want our relationships to become more harmonious and loving, we must set the intention—and then understand that our intentions (and the intentions of others) create the reality we experience. Every relationship, and every situation we find ourselves in, serves a purpose in our growth and evolution; therefore, we can trust that whatever we are experiencing right now is part of our healing journey.

Cherishment

For love to flourish, we must expand our limited concepts of love to something that is larger. When we take our wedding vows, we say to one another, "To love and to cherish…" But what exactly does it mean to cherish? Cherishment means we feel bathed in kindness, warmth, tenderness, and affection. There is a sweet indulgence in being cherished by another. Whereas food nourishes the body, being cherished nourishes the soul. When we are held in a deeply felt way, safe, protected, and cared for, we feel more than love, we feel cherished.

There is a sweet indulgence in being cherished by another.

A fundamental shift occurs in our relationships when we cherish one another's presence. Instead of projecting our habitual assumptions onto our loved ones, we begin to see them with fresh eyes. We shift from labeling each other as "husband" and "wife," or "mother" and "father," to looking at each other as human beings on a journey together. Jewish philosopher, Martin Buber, called this awareness a movement from "I-It" relationships to "I-Thou relationships." In I-It relationships everything and everyone, whether it is a piece of furniture or another person, is separate from us. But when we move to I-Thou—we exist in living relationships with everything and everyone around us. Barriers are broken down and in fact do not exist. When we see through the lens of I-Thou we see the sacredness in our relationships; we see unity and wholeness. We look at the ones we love knowing they are part of us, and we are part of them. We know that when we hurt another, we hurt ourselves. We understand that whatever we do to others, and whatever we think about others always comes back to us. As Buber said, I-Thou relationships are meetings with divinity, and the ultimate Thou is God.

When we cherish our partner, we can forgive him or her for not being as perfect as we would like. And then we can begin giving them loving attention. Their positive attributes will be easier to see when we stop focusing on all their faults. We can give them the opportunity to show us how wonderful they actually are. By withholding judgment (in our thoughts and our words) and looking for the good in our partner, we will find that he or she shows us more of it. In wabi sabi, we seek out the best in each other, not the worst, and by doing so, we show respect and honor to our humanness. When we feel loved and respected, imperfections and all, our love flourishes.

5 good things

Wabi sabi love requires us to regard ourselves as life-long learners in a class that never ends, and in a school that exists everywhere we go. As we learn, we improvise. We accept that we will fall down, cry, yell, and fall short of perfection. With time and experience we learn to love more gracefully and elegantly. We find ways to handle the hardships we encounter with more calm. Experience teaches us that saying "I do" is just the beginning of fostering closeness, passion, and commitment with another human being. When I see an old couple strolling down the street arm in arm, with a quiet smile passing between them, I glimpse what most of us desire—romance, friendship, and partnership in daily life. As much as we long to have this, we forget that in order to create these kinds of relationships in our life, we must first become the loving person we desire.

How can we create healthy, nourishing relationships? What does wabi sabi love look like in real life? Consider what Jean Baker Miller, M.D., author of the classic *Toward a New Psychology of Women*, defined as the five good things that characterize growth-fostering relationships that are empowering to all people. The first good thing is that you have a sense of zest or well-being that comes when you connect with another person. You feel energized and excited about life. Ask yourself, "Do I feel healthy and energized when I am with my partner (or potential partner)?"

The second good thing is that you feel productive—you have the ability and motivation to take action in the relationship and your life. You feel free to be yourself. There is a shared sense of decision-making and power in the relationship. Ask yourself, "In this relationship, do I feel like I can say and do what I want? Am I taking positive steps in other areas of my life as well?"

The third good thing is a sense of increasing clarity—you are growing in self-knowledge and knowledge about the other person through this relationship. There is mutual growth and exploration. Ask yourself, "Is there a spirit of curiosity and discovery in this relationship, of truly knowing and honoring the individual uniqueness of each person?"

The fourth good thing is that your sense of worth increases. When you feel loved and cherished, you will develop more self-confidence and feel valued for who you are. Ask yourself, "How do I feel about myself in this relationship? Am I loved for who I really am?"

Am I loved for who I really am?"

And the fifth good thing is that you desire more connections in your life, not less. You continue to spend time with friends and family, and engage in activities that you enjoy with others. Ask yourself, "Do I feel isolated in this relationship, or do I have good connections with other people too?" Creating a network of love and friendship is essential for every woman to flourish. In healthy, nourishing relationships, we feel loved and respected for more than our bodies or our minds—there exists a gentle reverence for the beauty of our soul.

The value of impermanence

A basic rule in wabi sabi is that nothing lasts forever. We cannot escape this truth. Everything we accomplish will eventually fade away. It might be depressing to think about how transitory our lives are, but learning to accept impermanence empowers us to cherish and enjoy what we have right now. When we know that we will experience loss we come to understand that what we have now is all the more precious, because it may be gone tomorrow. Learning to embrace the here and now—without lamenting the past or fearing the future—allows us to appreciate all the good in our life. Wabi sabi asks us to stop worrying about love; instead, welcome it when it comes, enjoy it while you have it, and let it go when it's over. Honor love's coming and honor love's going.

Honor love's coming and honor love's going.

Being aware of the impermanence of all things gives us the choice to respond to life in one of two ways: we can celebrate whatever good is before us here and now, or we can fret and worry over the unpredictable nature of life. When we choose to hold on to sadness or resentment from the past, we miss the present. And if we choose to worry about the future we miss the present as well. If we are not mindful, our life slips away, and we miss out on all the beauty along the way. Like a colorful and fragrant bouquet of flowers that will eventually die, wabi sabi teaches us to love in the now because that is all we truly have. Knowing this empowers us to treasure our relationships—to care for them like we would a special garden. When we plant our seeds in rich soil and make sure they get sun, water, and nutrients, there is a good chance that healthy flowers and vegetables will grow. The same is true in our relationships—we must nourish them if we want them to stay healthy and grow.

Modesty and humility

Modesty and humility are two words central to wabi sabi. When we approach our loved ones with honesty and openness, and listen to them, really listen to them, from the heart, with no false pretenses or personal agendas, we love the wabi sabi way. The ability to listen with your heart is an art few people have mastered. It requires us to be so genuinely interested and curious about the person we are with that he or she feels like the most important person in the whole world. It is a wonderful feeling when someone gives you their undivided attention and bathes you in the warm glow of their loving eyes. This is the gift of *presence*, when you are deeply listened to—mind, body, and soul.

Few things can heal our relationships faster than deeply listening to one another. When you are truly present your eyes say to your partner, "I see you, I truly see you." Your voice conveys, "I hear you, I hear what you are saying to me." And your physical presence expresses, "I am here for you, how can I show you my love and devotion?" Most of us live in a constant state of multi-tasking busyness. In order to truly listen to one another, we need to turn away from all the noise and give the ones we love our undivided attention. If we can allow the pace of our relationships to slow down to the pace of our hearts, we have a chance of finding the genuine understanding and love that is buried underneath all the distractions.

Julie Gohman, Ph.D.

How often do you listen to the ones you love in the way you would want to be heard? How often do you honor the truth of the other person even if it is different than your own? How often do you listen for the underlying feelings of what your partner said instead of getting defensive, criticizing, or voicing a snappy comeback? When we invite others to speak openly and truthfully, to share their experiences, feelings, and thoughts, and listen with sensitivity and awareness, we are practicing wabi sabi love. Every woman I know has voiced this need, "I wish he or she would just listen to me." First and foremost, we want someone to listen and acknowledge what we are feeling. The way to understanding each other is through deep listening—a practice that shows reverence, humility, and compassion. If we want this for ourselves, like everything, we must practice giving it to others. Wabi sabi teaches us that relationships bloom when we are willing to listen deeply to one another's truth and hold it gently in our hearts.

*Relationships bloom when we are
willing to listen deeply to one another.*

Naikan

Today, we live at a fast pace. The stress we feel on a daily basis often deters us from giving loving attention to our self and to our relationships. As women, we are experts at multi-tasking; we can change clothes, put on make-up, call our sister, make supper, and help the kids with homework all at the same time. The problem is, how many of these things are we doing well? We need to get rid of the distractions so we can find our way back to the sweet place in our relationships, to rediscover the beauty of our love. There is an important exercise in wabi sabi called *naikan* that can help.

The word *naikan* means, "to look inward." Naikan is all about tender soul-searching; it is to "see oneself through the eyes of the soul." The basis of this practice is to become reflective about yourself, your actions, and the repercussions that follow. The belief underlying naikan is that life holds an infinite amount of love and that when we observe things and experiences with loving eyes we begin to understand how blessed we are. We find freedom and peace of mind by focusing more on what we are giving instead of worrying about what we are getting.

For a taste of naikan, try the following exercise, which only takes 15 minutes. Find a time when you can sit alone in silence. Think of a key person in your life. It could be your mother, your partner, your child, or maybe a dear friend. You may have a good relationship with this person, or you may not. Ask yourself the following questions slowly, and allow yourself to reflect (and journal if you like) on the answers as they come: What has this person given me? What have I given this person? What difficulties have I given this person? Can I find gratitude for what this person has brought into my life? Don't rush through the process. Allow yourself the space and time to move beyond your ego into the territory of your soul. Open up to whatever comes. Listen to the shy voice inside you. Afterwards, it is good to offer forgiveness to yourself for the problems you may have caused, and then to offer forgiveness to the other person for the pain they may have caused. Let go of any blame, judgment, or anger. End your exercise by reflecting on what you have learned from this relationship. Let gratitude wash over you.

Naikan helps us peel back all the layers of who we are, and strip away the false ego. Through this practice, we move away from self-obsession toward humility and acceptance. Instead of becoming embroiled in our relationship drama, we step back and gain a larger perspective. Ultimately, we grow in awareness about ourselves and our relationships through naikan. We learn to accept things that we cannot change. It becomes clearer to us that if we want love, we have to give love. If we want peace, we have to become peaceful human beings. If we want serenity, we have to accept life as it is. When we serve life with humility, we also serve ourselves.

If we want peace, we have to become peaceful human beings.

Crinkled hearts

One day my youngest son came home from first grade with an unusual art project. It was a paper heart colored with crayon. The heart had been scrunched and crunched, and there were cracks and crinkles all over it. When I asked my son what happened to his beautiful heart, he looked at me solemnly with his big blue eyes. Then, in a very serious voice, he told me that our hearts get crinkled in real life when unkind and hurtful words are spoken. When we fight with one another, our hearts get more crinkles. And when we do not feel loved or have a sense of belonging our hearts crack. Once our hearts are crinkled and cracked, we can try to smooth them out, but they will never be the same again. Then my son grabbed his paper heart and ran over to the kitchen window and held it up as high as his little arms could reach. The light shined through all the cracks and the crinkles, transforming the heart into a beautiful work of art.

We affectionately called my son's first-grade teacher Ms. B. She became a teacher later in life and was passionately devoted to her young students. On her desk was a mountain of papers, projects, art supplies, and snacks that threatened to topple over at any moment. But that didn't matter because the students knew that Ms. B loved them. With her encouragement, they blossomed in her classroom. By using a simple art project, Ms. B. taught her students several invaluable lessons that day. First, we must try to be gentle and kind with one another because the wounds of the heart forever change us. Second, when our heart becomes cracked and crinkled—an inevitable part of the human journey, it does not subtract from the beauty of who we are. In fact, Ms. B taught her students that the places where we develop cracks and crinkles are often where we grow stronger and more beautiful. By keeping our hearts open and letting the light shine through, we dwell in love. Ms. B. did not use the words wabi sabi to describe the crinkled hearts—but it was wabi sabi.

Love is the most beautiful and precious part of being alive.

Wabi sabi love does not promise that everything in your relationships will turn out perfect. In fact, it is asking you to stop worshipping the illusions that create such unrealistic expectations. Wabi sabi reflects the very essence of Mother Nature in its simplicity. You would never expect the sea to always be calm and peaceful. There are waves, storms, and the water can be choppy and unpredictable. The sea may seem angry, chaotic, or even full of mischief at times. We are like that, and our relationships are like that too. The timeless wisdom of nature allows us to see that sometimes our relationships are sunny and wonderful, and sometimes they are dark and cold. Nature smells like springtime blossoms, and nature smells like a rotting log. In wabi sabi love, we embrace both—knowing that nothing is perfect, and nothing lasts forever.

Love is the most beautiful and precious part of being alive. It cannot be bought or sold; it must be freely given and graciously received. When we are mindful that the love in our life is a gift, we can choose to honor it every day. As one of my favorite authors, Leo Buscaglia, once said, "A life of love is one of continual growth, where the doors and windows of experience are always open to the wonder and magic that life offers. To love is to risk living fully."

> *The question to ask yourself is:*
> *Am I ready for wabi sabi love?*

For Wabi Sabi Love

*May you be blessed
with moments of clarity
when the veil lifts
and you see the beauty
of life as it is.*

*May you be blessed
with the courage
and strength
to be fully present
to all that life brings.*

*May you be blessed
with the wisdom
to be kind
a gift to those you meet
and to your true self.*

*May you be blessed
with a generous heart
and peaceful mind
open to forgiveness
and ready for wabi sabi love.*

Julie Gohman, Ph.D.

Am I ready for wabi sabi love?

The Third Sacred Question

Am I ready for wabi sabi love?

The Fourth Sacred Question

What Is True For Me?

*Now I become myself. It's taken Time,
many years and places....*
—May Sarton

Most of us want to know who we really are before we die. We want to discover what our shy soul has to say. We want to find the treasure that lies hidden within us and share it with the world. Like water that sparkles in the light, the truth of who we are can then shine clear and bright in our lives.

Finding our truth brings a harmony into our life that reflects a pure knowing about our essence. By listening to the voice of our soul, and speaking and acting from our center, we honor what is good and true and beautiful within us. When we do this, we feel the bliss of living a life that is faithful to our authentic and true self. Being true to our soul, therefore, is a pathway of healing, renewal and transformation for every woman.

For example, in the Greek myth of Eros and Psyche, Psyche is a pregnant mortal woman who is seeking to be reunited with her husband, Eros, the God of Love. But in order to be reconciled with Eros, she must complete four tasks that are given to her by Aphrodite, who happens to be Eros' angry and antagonistic mother. The first task that Psyche is given is to sort through a heaping pile of corn, barley, millet, chick peas, lentils, beans, and poppy seeds—all mixed together. She must sort out the seeds into separate piles by evening. Luckily, a troop of ants help Psyche, and she successfully completes the task before nightfall. Similarly, as women, we often need to sort out a jumble of conflicting feelings and thoughts. We must look inward and "sort the seeds." According to Jean Shinoda Bolen, M.D., author of *Goddesses in Everywoman*, this requires "that a woman look honestly within, sift through her feelings, values, and motives, and separate what is truly important from what is insignificant."

If we imagine our life as a precious lump of clay, we can understand that we are like a sculptor. We continually sculpt our life into shapes that reflect our beliefs, assumptions, and guiding principles. When there is harmony between what we believe and what we are living—when we honestly examine them and find they match—we are living our personal truth. And when we live our personal truth, there is no conflict in our soul, only peace. Our lump of clay is formed into a beautiful work of art that reflects our essence.

*When we live our personal truth,
there is no conflict in our soul.*

We all have an internal truth-tester. It is another "nose" we use to sniff out the people and places around us. We know when a situation is not right. We sense when someone is lying to us, and deep down we know when we are lying to ourselves. Sometimes we have to hit rock bottom, with nothing left to lose before we are willing to face the truth. But there is an easier way—we can open our heart, listen, and trust that our truth will emerge.

When we open our heart and listen closely, we can hear the voice of our soul that continually urges us to dwell in truth. It speaks to us. It prompts us to ask important questions, and it helps discern what is best for us. Our truth is like a song that resides in our heart. It is our job to discover the melody and sing along with it.

We can find our truth. We just need the courage to ask the questions. What are my real beliefs? And what are the beliefs that I have accepted that no longer resonate with me? What matters most to me? What do I really want? What enlivens me? What depletes me? What are the conflicting urges within my heart? These are not easy questions to answer. Be patient. The important thing is to begin the conversation.

The search for truth

There is no magic formula in the search for truth. Finding our personal truth is a process that unfolds slowly over time as we turn within and befriend the beauty of our own soul.

Most of the time, what we accept as truth—our beliefs, assumptions, and guiding principles—comes from our family of origin, our community, and our particular culture. Often we see or hear something over and over until we gradually believe it to be true. Many of us feel a gap between who we really are and the life we are living because of what we were told as a child. If we were not accepted and encouraged to be who we really are, we quite naturally learned to construct an outer persona that met the expectations of others. Inevitably this leaves us feeling hollow inside. In this gap is where we feel the conflict between our true self, our authentic presence, and the outer life we have constructed. When the tension becomes intolerable between who we are on the inside and the life we are living, it is time to begin the journey to discover what is really true for us. It is time to begin sifting and sorting through the seeds of our life.

The journey of finding our truth begins when we are willing to explore all that we currently believe to be true. These are like plants that have grown from the garden of our youth. Even after these plants have grown and taken hold, we can trace them back to their roots and decide if we want to keep these plants alive or pull them out and plant something new. We can ask ourselves: Do I want to continue nourishing this belief, or am I ready to dig it out and plant a new one? It takes time to discover what we have picked up from our friends, the media, pop culture, our family of origin, our belief systems, and the places we have lived, and then decide if it truly something we want to keep or get rid of.

Being truthful demands courage and honesty—with others and ourselves. It demands a willingness to contemplate life's deepest questions. As Rumi, the 13th-century Persian poet, says, "Lift your foot. Cross over. Move into the emptiness of question and answer and question."

Emotional honesty

It is difficult to find our truth if we are not consciously aware of our feelings and desires. Emotional honesty is the first step toward finding our truth, and it comes when we can recognize and validate our inner signals. Allowing

Julie Gohman, Ph.D.

ourselves to consciously feel what we feel, and to trust in those feelings, is emotional honesty. The problem is that many of us have fallen into the habit of stifling our natural self-expression and denying our truth.

When my children were little, I had a poster on our refrigerator that illustrated facial expressions and the emotions that go with them. Under the beaming smiley face, it said, "Happy," and under the face with tears it said "Sad." Every day we would look at the poster and point to the facial expression that matched how each of us felt. The goal was for my children to develop emotional awareness.

I bought the poster for my children, but soon discovered that it was I who needed it most. By nature, I have always been a positive and optimistic person, but I realized that I had learned to hide behind a smile, even when I was feeling down. I believe that posters like the one I had on my refrigerator belong in every home—not just for the children, but also for the adults who have become detached from their true emotions.

Personal truth demands that we reclaim our emotional honesty.

We often lose the ability to be emotionally honest during childhood. Many of us grow up in families in which no one knows how to feel or express all their emotions. How can they show us what it means to be emotionally honest if they don't know themselves? Sometimes certain emotions are frowned upon for girls. Gender stereotypes often send a message that it's okay for girls to be happy, but not angry. It's okay for women to be generous and kind but not assertive or self-confident. Many of us learn that emotional honesty is just not acceptable.

The search for personal truth demands that we reclaim our emotional honesty. We have to be brave enough to stop deceiving ourselves about how we feel. Many women fall into the trap of thinking that it is more spiritual to keep the peace and be quiet in contentious situations. As the caretakers and peacekeepers in our families, and in the world, we dampen our emotions too often. We imagine that it is more holy to not rock the boat, not to feel too much, not to get too excited, and not to make waves. But in doing this, we cut ourselves off from our passionate nature and our sense of being fully alive. We lose our connection to the wisdom of the heart and our own truth.

We need to give ourselves permission to feel everything.

Why do we erect walls around our heart, and deceive ourselves? Why do we choose to run away or hide from our emotional truth? These are often learned behaviors, but on some level we are also afraid. Fear stops us from tearing down the walls around our heart. Fear stops us from being completely vulnerable and open. We are unwilling to admit that something inside of us is cracking or breaking or hurting or weeping. Instead, we put on a brave face and ignored our feelings. We say everything is fine when it's not. We endure polite exchanges instead of having genuine conversations. We are wary of being hurt, rejected, abandoned, or worse. Rather than doing the soul work of discovering what is deep within us, we often choose to mask who we really are, and how we really feel. But the energy of being untrue can be felt, and we do not do ourselves, or the people in our lives, any favors when we deceive ourselves.

If we want to live with emotional honesty, we can no longer play it safe by suppressing our emotions and pretending to be happy when we are not. We need to give ourselves permission to feel everything. This requires a commitment to being present to our emotions at any given moment—simply to be with what is true. It also requires courage.

When we have the courage to allow ourselves to feel whatever arises, we experience our emotions as they flow through us. Sometimes our emotions pass through us quickly, coming and going in the blink of an eye, other times they seem to stick to us like thick mud.

The key to dealing with all our emotions is to engage them mindfully. We can acknowledge all our emotions without holding on to any of them for longer than is necessary. It is always tempting to cling to pleasant emotions and to condemn the painful ones to dark recesses, but this is simply an avoidance tactic that will eventually fail. Engaging our emotions mindfully means approaching them with a willingness to experience them all—whatever they are—the good, the bad, and even the ugly. We can enjoy our pleasant emotions, and still find the courage to deal with our pain and sorrow when they arise, knowing they will not last forever.

Awakening to emotional life

When we make a commitment to emotional honesty—to be present with our emotions, and to engage them mindfully—we can meet every feeling that arises in us with compassion. We will begin to realize that everything we feel is okay, and we can become comfortable even with the emotions that we do not like. Most importantly, we will come to welcome all of our emotions as little messages from the heart asking us to pay attention. This is awakening to our emotional life.

Opening ourselves to the full spectrum of emotions enables us to begin living wholeheartedly. When we live wholeheartedly, we are open and awake. We feel happier and healthier. Our heart becomes a tender heart. When something is wrong we can tune in and listen. We can ask for guidance, and have faith that when we follow our heart, good things will come.

The path to personal truth

Like the mystics and sages from the world's spiritual traditions have taught, the spiritual path exists within our daily life. We don't need to travel to the mountaintop, or sit under a tree to be enlightened. Our path to truth is one that we walk every day, in our family life, at our jobs, in our communities, and with our friends. It comes into being with all the little things we do, from the moment we get out of bed in the morning until we shut our eyes at night. Our journey begins wherever we are in our everyday life—this is where we will discover our personal truth.

Not long ago, I attended a writing workshop in New York City. Coming from the Midwest, I was dazzled by the intense pulse and the constant hum of activity that pervades every corner of "the city that never sleeps." It was magnificent.

On my last day in New York, I was the only passenger on the airport shuttle. Being the curious creature that I am, I struck up a conversation with the driver, Carlota. Carlota was a kind, friendly old soul, and her big smile was infectious. She had come to New York from Spain many years before, and she had been driving passengers like me around the city for decades, an unusual occupation for a woman.

Julie Gohman, Ph.D.

It was rush hour, and we were sitting in bumper-to-bumper traffic, yet Carlota remained calm. While we were in the middle of all the honking horns and rude drivers that cut in front of us, Carlota just kept talking, smiling, and laughing. I was impressed. I asked Carlota what her secret was for staying so cheerful in the midst of such chaos. She told me she had her own guidelines for driving—in New York or anywhere—that allowed her to navigate with ease. By this time, I had whipped out my notebook and was frantically writing down every word that she said. I had a feeling that it was no coincidence that I was stuck in New York City traffic with Carlota.

Carlota's first guideline was to pay attention to the signs on the road. She told me that the signs along the way are meaningful; they hold important information, and she takes them seriously because she wants to be safe. Her second guideline was to be observant of her surroundings. Carlota had developed a keen sense of awareness. She was alert and vigilant. She knew what was happening both inside and outside her vehicle. Indeed, I noticed that she was always looking around. By doing this, she was able to avoid accidents, go around things that were in her way, and see what was coming ahead.

Carlota's last guideline was to allow plenty of room between her car and the car in front of her. Wisely, Carlota knew that sometimes she would suddenly need to change direction, turn around, or take a different route. If she got too close to the car in front of her, she would lose the ability to make a change. Not only that, but driving too closely to other cars often leads to crashes, and Carlota wanted to avoid those at all costs. In the end, Carlota told me it was pretty simple; she just had to remember these three things, and she would be fine driving in New York

City, or anywhere. "After all," she said, as cars raced by us, "what's the rush?"

Although Carlota's guidelines were for driving, in a much larger sense, they represented Carlota's personal truth, and they informed her approach to navigating life. She reads and heeds the signs along the way, she pays attention, and she gives others space (for safety, and in case she needs to make a change). These guidelines are like a beacon of light that help Carlota stay safely on course and make her way to wherever she needs to go.

Living in truth

I thought about my conversation with Carlota for a long time after I left New York. She inspired me to think about the guidelines I have set for my life—as a mother, wife, teacher, writer, daughter, sister, and friend. What truths anchor me and help me navigate through the chaos in my life? Like Oprah writes on the last page of her magazine every month (the page I always flip to first when it comes in the mail), I needed to discover: "What do I know for sure?"

The window Oprah allows us to look through as she goes through the ups and downs in her life is one of the reasons why so many women relate to her. We can sense that she is being open and honest and vulnerable—not just in her private life, but in front of millions of people—and that takes a great deal of courage and emotional honesty. I admire women who shed their pretenses and just say it like it is. It may not pretty, it may not be what we want to hear, but it's real and true and honest. When we look to women who live authentically, true to their soul, what we see is that things are always in transition. Just when we think we have life all figured out something shifts, and we must begin again. Change is happening all the time, whether we embrace it or not. Even difficult situations, and changes we do not welcome are opportunities to dig deep and discover what is true for us.

Part of every woman's journey is to define for herself what is true—not forever, but right now.

Part of every woman's journey is to define for herself what is true—not forever, but right now. What worked for us five years ago, or even yesterday, may have radically changed. And that is okay. We don't have to justify or explain our truth to anyone. What matters is that we have peace and harmony about who we are and the life we are living. What other people think is irrelevant. If we want to live an authentic life, then the only voice that truly matters is our own.

Just as spirituality is the eternal search for wisdom, truth is an eternal conversation about what is sacred. Living in truth means we are in constant conversation with our true self, with the full awareness that the conclusions will keep changing. As we meet and revisit important issues in our lives, we must give ourselves the freedom to change our mind, follow our heart, and speak our truth.

Truth is an eternal conversation about what is sacred.

Speaking the truth

Telling the truth is a potent source of freedom. When we speak our truth, we are no longer concerned with disguising ourselves. And as we learn to welcome the voice of truth within us, we begin to experience harmony between who we are on the inside and how we live on the outside.

There is no reason to be meek or timid when it comes to speaking your truth. You can speak boldly and with confidence. As you say what is true for you, you can speak with love and passion, and yet without blame or judgment. Your truth is a reflection of who you are, not a reflection of anyone else. Listening to the voice of your shy soul and speaking your truth is an act of liberation. It allows you to live wholeheartedly because you are not holding back or hiding anything.

> *When your truth emerges,*
> *it will always lead toward wholeness.*

Speaking your truth with a fearless heart enables you to express who you really are, and in doing so you become a source of light for others who struggle to find their truth. When you care less about what other people think and more about staying true to your soul, you become very clear. Matching your words with what is true for you also frees up huge reserves of creative energy that were previously bogged down with deception. For many women, this becomes a time of rediscovering dormant creative passions and abilities, and finally having the courage to pursue long-held dreams and goals. This is a form of truth telling. You are saying to the world, "This is who I really am. This is what I love. This is what I know for sure."

Speaking from the soul can be difficult. It takes time to distinguish the voice of your soul and then speak from that inward center. But you will feel a sense of calm and peace when you find that place inside and allow it to guide you through life. The process requires a great deal of self-compassion as you let go of what is untrue. You must be ready to let certain things die so that your truth can be reborn.

When you gain a rock-solid sense of knowing of what is true for you—you can gather the strength and courage that is required to create a life that is harmonious with your soul. For some women, truth reveals an absolute certainty about their purpose in life, and they embark on a new career that is aligned with their soul's calling. Sometimes the truth brings a painful awareness about a relationship—it hits us and we know in our bones that it's over. Or perhaps the truth comes as a soft whisper that reminds you of something you have forgotten long ago, and now you are ready to begin reclaiming the lost pieces of yourself. When your truth emerges, it will always lead toward wholeness.

As we discover who we really are, what we want, why we are here, and what we believe, we will grow in compassion. Our struggle for truth is mirrored in the lives of millions of other women around the world. We are each on a sacred journey through womanhood, a spiritual path of our own making. And we can see how each person we meet is also going through the process of peeling away illusions, like the layers of an onion, to discover their own personal truth too. As we learn to establish our true voice, we also learn to respect and value the spiritual paths of others.

Consider what God said to Mechthild of Magdeburg, a medieval mystic who was emboldened to write about her mystical encounters with God, "My dear One, do not be overly troubled. No one can burn the truth."

The question to ask yourself is: What is true for me?

For Truth

May the subtle whispers of your soul
awaken your mind and heart
to the harmony that comes
from knowing what is good and true.

May you be blessed
with a gracious inner life
that is illuminated by
love and compassion.

May the waves of emotion
that flow through your body
be welcomed as the wise friend
who comes to serve you.

May you be enfolded with kindness
as you speak with honesty
and dwell in the sacred place
where freedom is eternal.

Julie Gohman, Ph.D.

What is true for me?

The Fourth Sacred Question

What is true for me?

The Fifth Sacred Question

How Can I Bring The Wild Feminine Alive?

The creative life is the soul's food and water.
—Clarissa Pinkola Estés

There comes a time in every woman's life when spiritual famine takes hold. We feel lost, confused, and unsure. The clock is ticking and the years are passing by. We find ourselves yearning and restless. We wonder, "Isn't there more to life?" When a woman feels this way, she is in throws of what has been called "divine discontent." It causes us to question who we are, what we want, and what we are going to do with the rest of our lives. Our soul is rumbling because we are hungry and thirsty for a return to what we love. We want to recover a sense of destiny and purpose. It is as Hildegard of Bingen, the Christian mystic said, we have a great need to bring the lushness, the moisture and greenness, back into our lives to replace the aridness that has taken hold.

Our wild feminine nature is what breathes life into our creative spirit. It inspires and propels us to do what brings joy to our soul. For each woman it will be different, but the underlying feelings are the same: pure delight and inspiration. You may feel a burst of energy when you arrange flowers in a vase, or whip up your signature salad dressing. Joy may come to your soul when you help someone in need, or inspire and uplift others. Perhaps you need to sing, dance, and move your body. Life itself is a deeply creative process and we are not separate from it. If you think you're not the creative type, think again.

*Our wild feminine nature is what
breathes life into our creative spirit.*

Every woman is deeply creative in her own wonderful way. Our work in this world is a powerful pathway to meaningful creative expression. The wild feminine infuses how we make a living, as well as what we do in our free time—both are essential. For example, my mother loves music and plays the drums in a coffeehouse band at the age of 68. A friend of mine studied architecture and enjoys sketching new home plans. My sister designs and sells baby carriers and cute little shoes for children. My mother-in-law is a baker and always has a delicious treat waiting for us. And after many years, my aunt returned to graduate school, fulfilling a lifelong dream. Whatever is joyful to you will be a blessing to the world because the energy behind it is divinely inspired. When you have a strong desire to create something, trust that you are being guided toward a path with purpose and joy. Your job is to figure out what feels creative to you—and then name it, claim it, and bring it alive.

*Whatever is joyful to you will also be a blessing to the
world because the energy behind it is divinely inspired.*

Problems surface when we don't nourish the wild feminine within us. It gets pushed underground, and we become susceptible to depression, anxiety, anger, resentment, and destructive patterns. For most women, the wild feminine becomes an afterthought to an already jam-packed schedule. Eventually, we find ourselves feeling stagnate, hollow, and empty, tired of giving to everyone but ourselves. We aren't completely miserable, but we aren't happy either. We have lost touch with our creative spirit. When this happens, the shadows of our soul usually have to take us deep down. And down we plunge until we encounter what it is we most need to learn to reclaim the lushness of life.

Having a sense of overwhelming disenchantment with life has something to teach us. Feeling lost and restless is a sign of the wild feminine inside yearning to be reawakened. If we are willing to pay attention to these signs, and learn from them, we will be led beyond the surface into the territory of deep questions. We need to ask ourselves: What brings me alive? What nourishes my creative spirit? What excites me? What delighted me as a child? What do I feel passionate about?

What brings me alive? What nourishes my creative spirit?

No matter how lost we feel we can reclaim the wild feminine inside us and the creativity that comes with it. As we return to our natural instincts, we will come back to life. Reawakening the wild feminine does not mean being irresponsible or selfish. It means remaking our life to reflect the creative beings that we are—so that what we love infuses what we do. We can then live more authentically and feel more joy in every moment. In order to get there, we must first do as Anne Sexton advises: "Put your ear down close to your soul and listen hard."

Reclaiming the wild feminine

Reclaiming our wild feminine nature does not mean being out of control. Being wild is about being connected to the natural, instinctive part of ourselves that knows what we need in order to feel alive. This part of us intuitively guides us toward a vibrant creative life. To become truly wild, we must go deep within ourselves and discover what it is that we need to express.

We are born with marvelous impulses and innate promptings that can guide us through life. This is the "seeking" system that is part of our human makeup, and it is as natural as breathing. It leads us effortlessly toward curiosity, adventure, playfulness, joy, and meaning.

We must go deep within ourselves and discover what it is that we need to express.

When we lose touch with our basic impulses we are no longer listening to our wild feminine nature, and our seeking system cannot function as it was intended to. Like a wild animal that has been taken into captivity, we become too domesticated. We lose our natural instincts to play, laugh, and explore. We become docile, compliant, and silent—we lose our power. When this happens, we also lose what scientists call our "flight instinct." Instead of running away from harm, we become confused, complacent, and we give up. This is called "learned helplessness," and it is one reason we stay in abusive relationships and toxic situations.

Our wild feminine nature is weakened when we suppress it. By pushing it underground, we unknowingly are turning away from our greatest strength. When we accept and adapt to this state of being, we lose our soul voice. This causes us to abandon what we love, what we believe in, and what we know to be true and right for us. This phenomenon is called "normalizing the abnormal," and affects women in all cultures across the globe.

As women, we have been conditioned to appear outwardly pleasing; anything less and we are given names that are derogatory. But no matter how outwardly pleasing we appear, the wild, powerful, and luscious aspects of ourselves are still bubbling and fermenting away in our depths.

How can I bring more joy into my life?

Sublimation of the wild feminine can give rise to a shadow life. When moments of stolen pleasure are the only scraps we allow ourselves we begin sneaking what we need to feel vibrant and alive. We sneak time with friends, time to dream, time to dance, time to paint, time to write, time to listen to music, or time to read juicy books. Sometimes we sneak things that are not good for us because we are desperate and starving, trying to fill a void in our life.

We know a rebellion is stirring in us when it becomes harder and harder to pretend to be happy. A grand scheme for freedom is being hatched in the shadows of our soul. Something inside is growing tired of all the sneaking around and wants to be liberated.

At some point in every woman's life the wild feminine nature can no longer be repressed. It demands our attention. If we are honest with ourselves, we recognize there are broken places that need to be healed. And if we are brave, we make positive changes that feed our creative spirit.

It is never too late to return to our instincts and reclaim our wild feminine nature. But it requires a willingness to ask ourselves difficult questions, and a willingness to hear the answers—no matter what they are. If we are unhappy, we must ask: How can I bring more joy into my life? Who is responsible for my happiness? What is most important to me? If we are sneaking moments of stolen pleasure we must ask: Why do I feel that I have to grovel, plead, and sneak a life that is my own to begin with? How can I start standing up for what I need and want? If we have self-destructive habits, we must ask: Why am I hurting myself? How can I start loving myself more?

We must meet the challenges and hardships of reclaiming the wild feminine with courage and honesty. We will find the strength and stamina to be joyful and vibrant women if we take time to honor what brings us alive and feels deeply creative and nourishing.

Nurturing the wild feminine in a sacred circle

Once we have found the courage to face the shadows, we can nourish the wild feminine by creating a sacred circle of support. A sacred circle is a community that allows us to express ourselves with passion. It is a place where we feel safe, strong, loved and liberated. To quote feminist author Starhawk, it is, "A circle of healing. A circle of friends. Someplace where we can be free."

To give yourself the best chance for keeping your wild feminine nature alive and well, you must choose wisely when you are creating your sacred circle of support. What other people think and say can greatly affect you. It is crucial that you distance yourself from people who are not good for you. If someone is always belittling, criticizing, condemning, provoking, or dismissing you, that person is toxic. If you feel exhausted after spending your precious time with someone—in person or on the phone—that person is toxic. If you feel emotionally or physically unsafe around someone, that person is toxic, and dangerous. Ask yourself: Do my friends and family honor and cherish who I am, or do they cut me down? Do I feel healthy and happy around the people I spend time with, or are they poisonous to my soul?

As we reclaim the wild feminine from the shadows, we cannot forget that it is still quite fragile. We have to be cautious to safeguard this beautiful gift inside us. Julia Cameron, author of the best-selling classic *The Artist's Way*, tells us that we must stop the tortuous tango with the "crazymakers" in our life. We need to start dancing with friends who encourage us, believe in our creative spirit, and treasure who we are. In other words, if we want to nurture and protect our joy and well-being, we must leave the crazymakers outside our sacred circle of support.

Reclaiming your wild feminine nature can be an arduous journey. When you begin, you may find that some people will pressure you not to pursue what you love. In fact, they may do everything they can to keep you from doing so. Their fear of change will create challenges in your relationships. Don't let them stop you. You may be shunned and treated with hostility by a culture that does not honor a woman's soulfulness. Be brave and continue on. As your heart awakens to the wild feminine, and you discover how good it feels to nourish your creative spirit, you will become powerful in your own right. You will show others how to fall in love with life.

The wild feminine and the creative spirit

When we reclaim our wild feminine heart our creative spirit blooms. We no longer have to sneak time for what we love. We are finally free to practice our arts openly, and try new things that interest us. When we nourish our creativity, we reinforce our vital connection to the spirit of the divine that flows through us.

It can still be a challenge to establish the habit of allowing ourselves the freedom, time, and space we need to explore our creative passions. With busy schedules and people who need us night and day, it can feel nearly impossible at times. We must remind ourselves that by feeding our creative spirit, we become joyful, and that joy spreads to our families, coworkers, and everyone we meet. Our own radiant presence is a beautiful gift to others.

What follows are 10 things you can do to open the space in your life and your heart to nourish the wild feminine inside you. In no particular order of importance, they are: let loose, feed your soul, dwell in possibilities, find balance, be willing to receive, become fierce, plan artist dates, make a "Do Not Disturb" sign, take the leap, and continue soul-spinning.

Let loose

Letting loose our wild feminine nature is the first step to realizing the full extent of our creative spirit. This does not mean getting drunk or dancing on tabletops. It means listening hard to the wild feminine inside you. Letting loose is about freeing yourself from the inhibitions that hinder you from experiencing the beauty of your creative spirit. Maybe someone told you that you're not the creative type. Maybe you doubt that you have any talent. Maybe you have never let yourself be playful. It is time to let go of these ideas and begin anew.

When we let ourselves pursue our creative passion, whatever it may be, we are swept into the flow of joy. We lose track of time. We are infused with new ideas, and we are filled with inspiration. When this happens, the shackles of limitation begin releasing their hold on us. We discover the nature of our particular genius when we stop trying to conform to other people's expectations, and instead focus on what brings our spirit alive.

Feed your soul

A well-fed soul nourishes our creativity and strengthens our wild feminine heart. When we are fed real soul food, we become the wild and wise woman we were born to be.

There are four basic categories of soul food: time, passion, belonging, and sovereignty. These are essential for nourishing the wild feminine inside us. By giving ourselves time to pursue our creative interests, we stay connected to our passion. When we feel passion, we are experiencing the divine coursing through our veins. As we come alive, we discover our unique presence. We come home to our true self, and we belong in a way that feels perfect. Belonging restores our natural sovereignty. We feel supremely powerful over our own life.

Allow yourself generous servings of soul food. As you bravely express who you truly are, courage will become your badge of honor. It will carry you through your daily life as you feed your children, go to work, and do what you must do. When the wild feminine within you is nourished, you will be infused with the energy to face whatever life brings to you.

Dwell in possibilities

When we think there is only one way we should feel, or one way we should act, we are stifling and censoring our life—we are shutting down our unique and individual creative expression. We must lose the idea that there is only one way to be, and allow our creative spirit to show us the way. The more we listen to our heart and soul, and dwell in possibilities, the stronger and wiser we become.

When you let your creative spirit guide you, it is much easier to see that you always have choices. You can do something or not do something; you can choose this path or that path. You can go along with tradition or discover a new way. You can use your imagination to see where you want to be and how you might get there. When you realize that you always have choices you reclaim the power to make decisions, set goals, and focus on what you want to create in your life.

Dwelling in possibilities liberates us. It gives us the potential to see the life we want to create. If we seize the opportunities that come our way—with the awareness that our life is our own for the making—there is no limit to what we can accomplish.

Find balance

Putting all our energy into taking care of others—at home or work—leaves us no energy for nourishing ourselves. We must find a balance between our responsibilities to others and our responsibility to our creative life and our true self.

It is too easy to spend all our waking hours consumed with caring for the needs of others—children, parents, friends, partners, and employers all demand our time and energy. We want to care for the ones we love and do the best we can for those around us, but problems arise when we forget to nurture and care for ourselves too. An exhausted and depleted mother, friend, or employee is not the best mother, friend, or employee she can be. We need to set limits and create boundaries that help us stay happy and healthy.

Taking time for our creative life is restorative. It replenishes the energy we need to meet all the demands placed on us, and all the demands we make of ourselves. When we establish a healthy balance in our life—between what we need for ourselves and what others need from us—everyone benefits. A balanced life does not come easy, and what it means to you may not be what it means to me. It requires us to establish firm limits, examine our priorities, and make changes when they are needed.

Try not to let the nagging voices—in your head, and in the world around you—stop you from allowing your creative life to blossom. Exercise your personal freedom to experience the joy that comes from nourishing your soul. And in return, your creative life will give you the energy, strength, and stamina you need to flourish as a woman in this world.

Be willing to receive

Women are givers. We are born and raised to be generous with our time, talent, and affections. But when it comes time to receive, many of us have trouble. Instead of welcoming the good that is trying to come our way, we often reject it. We must learn to accept all the blessings that come into our life with gratitude. By learning to receive graciously, and not just continuing to give to others, we can hear the whispers of our soul again, letting us know that our creative spirit is worthy of time and attention. Our wild feminine nature is still alive.

If you think about the divine as a great hostess, you can see that accepting and appreciating all the gifts you are offered honors the divine. When someone compliments you, learn to say "thank you" graciously, and take the compliment. If your partner offers to cook, or do the laundry, or watch the kids for an afternoon or evening—so you can work on a project, or finish that book you are reading, or take a bubble bath—learn to say, "Thank you sweetheart. That would be great." You can learn to accept and appreciate the gifts of time, energy, and devotion from others who want to support and help you.

It is simple, really. When help and support are being offered, learn to say "yes" more and "no" less. When the divine brings good into your life, accept the gift and show your appreciation. The more love and support you let into your life, the more love and support you can offer to others. It becomes a wondrous cycle of giving and receiving that never ends.

Become fierce

Once we have found the courage to listen to the wild feminine inside us, we have to take care not to let it slip back into the shadows. We already know how it feels to be empty and exhausted, to sleepwalk through our days. We do not ever want to feel that way again. To avoid becoming a starved and miserable soul, we must be fierce about protecting the time and space we need for our creative life.

When we have the courage of our convictions, we can stand-up for ourselves. We do not have to feel guilty for taking time to follow our creative passions. Like a lioness protecting her cubs, we must fiercely defend our creative life as if the future depends on it—because it does. A starved and miserable soul is practically useless to those who depend on her, and she can be a danger to herself. We must be strong in the knowledge that when we nourish ourselves we flourish as mothers, lovers, daughters, sisters, and friends. Everyone benefits when we are fierce about protecting our creative spirit.

You cannot let any thought, person, or problem stand in the way of becoming the vibrant, creative, and unique woman you are meant to be. The gift of your creative spirit is a legacy of love to those around you. When you protect and nourish your wild feminine nature, every area of your life will bask in the glow of your creative light.

Plan Artist dates

Cameron approaches creativity as a spiritual process, and she recommends what she calls "the artist date." This is a block of time you set aside to be playful. Think of it as a play date with your inner artist.

An artist date is not meant to be productive; it is meant to be fun. No one other than your inner child is allowed to attend. Anything that feels playful counts as an artist date. Playing with your dog, going to a movie, visiting an art gallery, writing a story, or laying in the grass and making shapes in the clouds could all be artist dates. Think about mystery, not mastery. Mystery intrigues us and leads us to new discoveries; it piques our curiosity and enriches our creative spirit.

Learning how to play again will give you a new surge of energy that feels wonderful. You might feel like a kid again. Your mind will become more inventive. Your body will be filled with excitement. As you play, you are replenishing your inner well—your reservoir of abundance and joy for life.

Make a "Do Not Disturb" sign

Making a "Do Not Disturb" sign is one of the easiest and most practical things you can do to nourish your creative spirit. Get out the paper and the paint, or the cardboard and the Sharpies. Scribble "Do Not Disturb" and make sure to use it often.

It is difficult for most of us to set boundaries and stick to them. We cave, we doubt, we feel guilty, we get sidetracked and distracted, and then we do not get any time to ourselves. How often do you set aside even an hour a week to nourish your creative spirit? How often do you protect your time and energy for doing what you love? Give yourselves permission to abandon everything—even if it is only for just a few moments—for a chance to come alive.

Make no apologies, be firm, plan ahead, prepare everyone, and then go and do something that fills you with joy. Walk away from the laundry, forget the "to do" list, leave the phone behind, hang up the "Do Not Disturb" sign, close the door, and enjoy your creative time.

Take the leap

We are often fearful to try something new, nervous we will disappoint others, afraid we will fail, or hesitant to begin again. When fear steers our life, it holds us back from all the wonderful possibilities that exist for us. We must put our fears to rest, take a leap, and venture into the unknown. When we do this, we will find exciting new opportunities everywhere. Becoming fearless gives us wings.

When we leap into the unknown—with a new project, a new job, a new relationship, a new city, a new house—we find untapped reserves of creative energy flowing through us. We are taken to unforeseen places in our heart. It does not matter if we are not fantastically successful at everything. Many things will not work out at all, and that is okay. In fact, it is to be expected. The important thing is to put ourselves out there, try, accept that we might fail, and be ready to do it all again. As Anaïs Nin writes: "Life is truly known only to those who suffer, lose, endure adversity and stumble from defeat to defeat."

Sometimes we reach a roadblock in life, or something ends, and our very survival depends on our ability to begin again. If we have lost our job, home, or significant relationship, there is no time for fear or excuses or stagnation. Life goes on, and we have to start over. If we do not learn how to swim, we will drown in our misery. This is when we need to reach deep inside ourselves and find the courage to keep going. When we have no choice but to begin again, we must firmly take our fears in hand and go forward—trusting that we will find our way through the darkness.

A woman who is willing to pick herself up, dust herself off, and begin again—not just once, not just twice, but every day—is a woman who is gloriously and courageously alive. Knowing that she was brave enough to take leap after leap into the unknown and that she lived her life to the fullest, she will smile on her deathbed and have no regrets.

Continue soul-spinning

Soul-spinning means doing little things to keep our creative spirit alive—even if we cannot go full steam ahead right now.

We can do something related to our creative passion every single day. For example, you may love to paint, but have no time. Maybe you take out your paints on Monday and arrange all the supplies. On Tuesday, you begin dreaming about the picture you want to paint. On Wednesday, you make a sketch. On Thursday, you begin mixing the paints. And on Friday you take your children to your sister's house and paint to your heart's delight. For every woman it will be different, but the point is to find some way of keeping your creative spirit engaged and curious so it doesn't wither and die.

If we stop taking time for what we love we banish the wild feminine from our soul. It is up to us to nurture our creative spirit in some way every day so that it will not starve and fade away. As a writer, there are days when the only writing I do is scribbling one word on a sticky note, but that is enough to keep it going until the next day. It keeps the fire smoldering until I can bring it back to a roaring blaze. No one else is responsible for minding our creative spirit. We alone must choose to give it something each and every day.

If we love ourselves, we must continue soul-spinning. Our wild feminine nature will come back to life when we commit to keeping the creative fire burning in small ways, in fleeting moments, every day of our life.

The question to ask yourself is:
How can I bring the wild feminine alive?

Julie Gohman, Ph.D.

For The Wild Feminine In You

May you be blessed
as your soul unfurls
awakening to the adventure
of the creative path.

May the light that fills you
emerge in wild and wondrous ways
as you become your heart's desire
and hold nothing back.

May your delight unlock the dreams
that whisper inside you
as your senses discover the bliss
of living with passion.

May you be touched by grace
and filled with courage
as you answer the call
of your wild feminine nature.

The Fifth Sacred Question

How can I bring the wild feminine alive?

Julie Gohman, Ph.D.

How can I bring the wild feminine alive?

The Sixth Sacred Question

Do I Have The Gift Of True Friendship?

> *Friendship with oneself is all important,*
> *because without it one cannot be friends*
> *with anyone else in the world.*
> —Eleanor Roosevelt

In contemporary societies, women no longer have the same access to the support systems and networks that our mothers and grandmothers took for granted. Many of us have never been members of a sewing circle or a knitting group, and I would bet that many of us have never participated in a quilting bee. Our families are scattered across states and countries, and our lives are busier than ever before. We have become lost to each other. Despite the fact that many of us yearn for deep, soulful connections with other women, for the laughter and tears that come when we share our lives, we live in a world that invalidates true friendship among women. Here's the truth: when women form circles of friendship and belonging with one another,

Julie Gohman, Ph.D.

they create sister-bonds that infuse their lives with hope, healing, and happiness. When a woman has a sister by her side, she can watch her career sink, her marriage fall apart, her children leave home, and her dog die, and she will survive. When a girlfriend stays with you through the best and the worst times of your life—that is part of the love that makes you whole.

True friendship is a precious gift and a beautiful presence in our life. Friends offer safe harbor when the sailing gets rough. They become a mirror to reflect back to us who we are when we have lost our way. People with whom we can share our true feelings, crazy ideas, deepest fears, and tragic sorrows grace us with a priceless treasure that sustains and heals us. We are nurtured by their unconditional acceptance and warm regard. When we have good friends (including the furry, four-legged kind) we feel a quiet happiness that fills our soul. We know we are not alone. Our lives are enriched by the give and take we experience in these circles of belonging, and they bring us the connections we need to feel loved and cherished.

True friendship is a precious gift.

Before we can find the kind of friendship we desire, we must think about whom we choose to allow into our life. Inviting people into our circle who do not have our best interests in mind will only create disharmony and distrust. Therefore, we must witness how others behave, what they say, and if they treat people (and animals and the earth) with kindness and respect. This will give us a good idea of how they will treat us. Trust in any relationship must be earned over time. We can tune into our intuition, our inner guidance, to determine who to let into our life. There will be times when we need to walk away from someone. Give yourself permission to let go of friendships that no longer nourish you. Instead, find kind, loving, generous, and trustworthy people to be with. True friendship will always empower, inspire and help you become the radiant woman you were born to be.

In a universal sense, all women are daughters, mothers, and sisters, and we can reach out to one another to give and receive the precious gift of friendship. Busy as our lives are, we have to find new ways of nurturing our bonds of sisterhood. Whether we take a class, join a book club or volunteer in our community, we can connect with other women. Our physical, emotional, and spiritual well-being blossoms when together we feel the larger presence of the divine feminine that unites us.

Before we can reach out and find the friendship we desire, we must befriend our true self. When we accept who we truly are, we are ready to accept others as we find them. True friendship blooms when we recognize our own unique and special presence, and then offer it to another.

Befriending your true self

Learning to love ourselves deeply and completely—and learning to befriend our true self—is essential for every woman. We must understand that we, as much as anyone, deserve our own affection and love. Befriending our true self is the key to opening to real friendship with another human being.

When we feel lost and alone we stumble upon one of the greatest lessons of the soul. It is during bleak times that we are called to rediscover the wellspring of love within us. This is an eternal echo from the divine that acknowledges our worthiness, our beauty, and our belonging just as we are. Rather than growing bitter or hardening our hearts when we experience loss and pain, we can awaken to the miracle of friendship with ourselves. We can bring a gentle reverence and a soft kindness into our life by learning to love, treasure, and befriend our true self.

Befriending oneself comes when we love ourselves as the human beings we are, knowing we are perfectly imperfect. When we accept whatever we are going through, and whatever we are feeling—without heaping on self-judgment and criticism—we are learning how to befriend ourselves. Just as a dear friend would offer us their steadfast presence and understanding, we can turn within and offer ourselves love and compassion. Friendship with oneself takes hold when we care less about what other people think and more about finding peace within ourselves.

Solitude becomes a pathway to your own deepest belonging.

As you grow in friendship with your true self, you discover that time spent alone is nourishing to your soul. You become comfortable with your own presence and do not cling to others. There is no desperate attempt to always be with someone because you like your own company. Solitude becomes a pathway to your own deepest belonging. You are not lonely because you are at home with yourself. You are led to a realization: The deepest things that you need are not outside yourself; they exist within the circle of your own soul.

There is a wonderful welcome when you come home to yourself. In solitude, away from the obsessive images of womanly perfection, you come upon your own beauty, the radiant illumination of your soul. You find the treasure that you have been hopelessly seeking elsewhere. The blessings you used to crave from others—love, approval, and acceptance— now come from the eternal place within you. Solitude and silence become a lovely gift to yourself that nourishes, strengthens and renews you. Every woman who has befriended her true self knows—solitude is luminous.

Friendship with ourselves is about nourishing who we are so we can get up each morning and shine our divine light. When we honor who we are, and love our true self, we free our soul. The light within us grows bright and expresses itself in joyful ways. Instead of empty hands and heart, we radiate love and well-being, and it overflows naturally with gifts and blessings for others. We begin living with soul-fullness. From this fullness, we have more to give to the ones we love and the world around us.

When we learn to love and befriend our true self, we can love and befriend others. We are no longer needy and dependent, driven by external longings, because there is a secret equilibrium in our soul that radiates well-being and wholeness. As our light shines brightly from this place of friendship within ourselves, we become a friend who uplifts and encourages others.

Cherishing *anam caras*

We meet many fair-weather friends in life. These are the people happy to tag along for the good times, happy to take everything we have to offer, but once the going gets tough they evaporate like the dew on a hot summer morning. When we meet a real friend—someone who sticks by us no matter what—we are truly blessed. Real friends should never be taken for granted. But even among this very select group we will find greater treasures, we will find our *anam caras*.

Julie Gohman, Ph.D.

Anam Cara is an old Gaelic word that comes from the Celtic tradition, meaning "soul friend." The Celts believed in the spiritual dimension and saw the divine in every aspect of life—including the bonds of friendship. True friendship between two people that love one another was considered incredibly precious—it was a deep and sacred connection. The Celtic people were very loyal to family and tribe. They also appreciated the skills of gifted musicians and storytellers, and that is how their ancient understanding of soul friendship was preserved. To have an anam cara, according to the Celts, means you have a person to whom you can reveal the hidden intimacies of your life. This person becomes the true mirror to reflect your soul.

We exist together with our anam cara in a sacred circle of belonging at the soul level, and we accept each other unconditionally. We can reveal our mind and heart to our anam cara, and we have no need for disguises or posturing. Our friendship goes beyond the superficial, and it is not affected by distance or time. We can travel the world, and our anam cara is still with us. We can go for years without seeing our anam cara, and yet we pick up as if no time has passed when we see each other again.

Most of us have had the experience of meeting someone for the first time and feeling as if we have known him or her for a lifetime. We just click. We like each other instantly, we are comfortable with each other, and we let our guard down immediately. We seem to recognize ourselves in each other, and we quickly become trusty companions and confidants. This is the kind of friendship that gives wings to all of the possibilities within us. Our anam cara blesses us with the rare understanding that makes us feel at home. We rest in the shelter of our friendship. The soul-bond that we share reflects the beauty that is possible when two hearts nurture and embrace one another. This is the ancient and eternal light that exists with the "friend of your soul."

When you meet your anam cara, you know a sacred gift has come into your life. Share yourself, learn from them, and appreciate the sacred bond that you have, for you will not experience this with many people. We must never forget to love and cherish the friendship of our anam caras. Often, we feel the pressure to attend to the "facts" of our lives—how much money we make, how big our house is, what we look like. Doing instead of being absorbs our energy. The Celtic concept of soul friendship would have us less concerned about what we should do, and where we should go, and what we should have, and more concerned about *how* to be—how to be a loving friend, how to nourish our sacred connections with others, how to love ourselves completely.

When you meet your anam cara,
you know a sacred gift has come into your life.

Originally, in the Celtic tradition, the word anam cara also conveyed the idea of one who was a spiritual guide, teacher, or mentor. It was considered essential that every person have a soul friend in whom there was absolute trust. Your anam cara should be someone who inspires you, listens to you—someone who sees you with "the eyes of the heart," as the early Irish writers would say. It means more than just seeing with the heart though; it also implies the ability to listen with the heart too. When you have an anam cara who comes from the heart, they can see your potential, and they believe in you, even when you have lost your way. Your anam cara always fosters your greatness.

St. Brigit, one of the most well known patron saints of Ireland, said that everyone needs a soul friend. Our soul friends remind us we are on a sacred journey. They help us celebrate who we are. Having an anam cara means we have a friend who encourages us, shows us compassion, and believes in our dreams and intuitions. We feel stronger and more confident when we have the gift of soul friendship in our lives.

Friendship with Other Women

The results of my research about women suggest that friendship with other women is one of the most important factors for happiness and well-being. But this is something most women already know. Deep in their heart they know much their soul sisters mean to them. Many of the women I interviewed said their girlfriends were the reason they made it through hard times. They were the lifelines when things got tough, and they needed someone who understood what they were going through. Without the gift of friendship, these women said they felt isolated and alone. No matter what the challenges were in these women's lives, there was a deep sense that when they had the support of a girlfriend, sister, or mother, life was more fulfilling. There was more joy and laughter and the heartbreaks were easier to bear.

We need someone who we can trust by our side.

In the lives of many women today, there is a great need for mentoring, for women to reach out to one another in friendship and wise counsel. When we encounter roadblocks in our life, and fall down on our knees in despair, we need someone who we can trust by our side. Such soul friendships can truly be life saving. Think of a critical time in your life when a mentor or guide (perhaps a teacher, relative, or good friend) helped you make a big decision. Perhaps they renewed your sense of hope for the future or made you laugh when you felt like crying, or helped you see your amazing potential. Sadly, many of us can remember times in our life when we needed the presence of a wise woman, but had no one. The reality is, in today's world, most women lack adequate mentoring. Many times we find ourselves lost, confused, and alone, unsure of which way to turn or what to do next. Finding even one person who we can trust to validate the meaningfulness of our existence is critical for us to flourish as women.

Our soul friends remind us we are on a sacred journey.

We can read books, and follow the directions of spiritual masters and mystics, but it is no substitute for having a living mentor and guide. If you have someone in your life that sees you, loves you and believes in you, someone you can entrust all the secrets of your heart, you are indeed blessed. Treasure your relationship, and treasure your anam cara. If you would like to find a mentor or guide, know that such a person exists for you, just waiting to be discovered. You may need to do some exploring to find your anam cara. Reach out and seek what you are missing. Sometimes when you are least expecting it, and most needing it, someone will come into your life and you will find a shelter for your soul.

A good place to start on the path to creating soulful connections in your life is by remembering that we must extend friendship to others if we want it for ourselves. Smile, open your heart, and let people in. Be present to the women in your life. Slow down and plan time in your busy schedule to do fun things with them. Pay attention when they are talking. Ask deep questions. Talk about your hopes and dreams. Move beyond the surface and get to know others more intimately. Be authentic—when you are real others will be drawn to you because they can sense that you aren't hiding under layers of disguise. The possibility for true friendship exists all around you. You simply need to reach out and share your beautiful presence with others. Like a magnet, you will attract the friendship you radiate.

Beautiful things happen when we connect as sisters and friends in this world.

Likewise, every woman can become a mentor, imparting the blessings of soul friendship to another woman in need. Beautiful things happen when we connect as sisters and friends in this world. Think of someone who may be in your life right now that may need your guidance. Mentoring requires that you make a heartfelt commitment, so choose wisely. Now, more than ever, we need to both give and receive the gift of true friendship to one another, so that as women we can stand strong and live with courage, wisdom, and joy.

A circle of fairy friends

Friendship is not only a circle of belonging where we are loved and accepted; it is also a source of great happiness in our life. When we gather with good friends we eat, we drink, and we laugh. We let our hair down and can be ourselves. We experience the energy of the fairies, what the Celtic tradition considered to be the energy of playfulness, frolic, laughter, and fun. The circle of friends that allows us to get outside ourselves and forget our everyday worries and concerns is a circle of fairy friends. We all need this respite and succor to replenish our soul—to play and giggle and be silly—even if it is only for a short time now and then.

Today's world has largely lost the magic of the fairies. Laughter and playfulness have given way to seriousness, productivity, efficiency, achievement, and acquisition. But we all need the magical energy of the fairies to lighten the load and make us smile. Being silly frees us from the illusions of control and self-importance. Little children embody the energy of the fairies—they play with abandon, laugh at everything, and do not worry about tomorrow. Little children are some of the best teachers on the planet for those of us who have become too serious and stuffy. They know the healing power of being ridiculously silly.

> *Being silly frees us from the illusions*
> *of control and self-importance.*

While the Celts believed the world of fairies was in another dimension, one that was invisible, they felt the presence of fairies in the green hills, woods, and water all around them. The fairies reflected whatever conditions the people found themselves in. In Ireland, where the Celts lived happy lives in a beautiful and serene environment, the fairies were happy too. They described the fairies as the "good people." And in places where life was harsher, the fairies were said to be fierce. Like the Celts, we can keep alive this magical spirit world by nurturing our friendships. When we take time out of our busy lives to play and have fun together, it is indeed like entering another dimension, one where time slips away. And that is when we have discovered the secret sparkle of fairies.

If you are lucky enough to have a circle of fairy friends—and the soul bond of an *anam cara*—you are truly blessed with good fortune. If instead you feel a hole in your life, and long for friendship, know that life will continue to give you opportunities to find friendship wherever you are. Commit to befriending your true self, and then, as if by magic, you will attract the perfect friends into your circle. It is never too late to find the joy and happiness that true friendship brings.

The question to ask yourself is:
Do I have the gift of true friendship?

For True Friendship

*May your life be filled
with the strength
and joy of women
who stand by your side.*

*May you learn to give
the precious gift
of friendship
to your true self.*

*May you always know
the love that comes
in the shelter
of your anam cara.*

*May you be blessed
with the sparkle
and mischief
of fairies.*

*May your treasure
include those
who are with you
through all things.*

Do I have the gift of true friendship?

The Sixth Sacred Question

Do I have the gift of true friendship?

The Seventh Sacred Question

What Is My Body Trying To Tell Me?

Before you speak...your body speaks for you.
—Isabelle Anderson

Back in the 1940's, a brilliant woman named Karen Horney, one of the founders of humanistic psychology, argued that people cope with their anxieties (caused by feeling unsafe, unloved, and unvalued), by disowning their real feelings and developing elaborate defenses. This is not just a psychological phenomenon, but a physical one as well. Horney claimed we tend to move *toward*, *against* or *away* from other people. Nowhere is this more evident than in our body. When we like someone, we lean in. When we feel angry or resentful, our body stiffens and prepares to fight. And when we have no desire to be around someone, we instinctively recoil, turn our body, or put space between us and the other person. Our body does not lie. Our hopes, fears, and desires, everything we truly like or don't like, everything that is good for us or not good for us, can be discovered by listening to our body. When we live fully attuned to our body, we can make wise decisions. We embrace our creativity. We know who we are. We feel good about ourselves. We trust our intuitions. And we say yes to love and pleasure.

Dr. Rosemarie Anderson, Ph.D., who I affectionately call my "transpersonal mama," was my academic advisor and chair of my research committee when I was in graduate school. She spent decades studying intuition and body intelligence, and pioneered research methods for the social sciences. She also developed an assessment tool for body awareness called the Body Insight Scale (go to mindgarden.com for more information). She teaches us that there are at least three forms of body awareness, or ways that we can listen to our body.

Comfort Body Awareness means we feel comfortable with our body, and we feel comfortable in the world. This is when we feel centered, and "at home" in our body and our surroundings. Ask yourself, where in the world do I feel most grounded, centered and at home in my body? With whom do I feel most comfortable and safe? Whose presence makes me uncomfortable (even if there is no rational reason)? When do I feel unsafe?

Inner Body Awareness means we recognize changes within our body like fatigue or a headache, or physical responses to certain emotions or environments. Ask yourself, when does my body shut down? Do I listen when my body sends me messages that it needs a change, or rest, or movement, or something different to eat? Where does my body feel most alive and happy? What happens in my body when I am afraid, anxious, overwhelmed, or sad?

Energy Body Awareness means we use our five senses and the body as a whole to respond to energy felt both inside and outside of our body. Sometimes known as the "vibe scale," it refers to those feelings we have of being balanced or unbalanced in our body, such as when we feel waves of energy around us or in us. We pick up "vibes" that tell us a situation or place is either safe or unsafe. Ask yourself, when have I felt something so strongly I couldn't ignore it, and it helped me out of a dangerous situation? How do I know when a person or place is safe and good for me? Do I listen when I get "vibes" about things?

"Does my body respond with a thud or a ping?"

The rewards are great when we become attuned to our body. Our physical well-being, safety, comfort, and ability to flourish, in fact, depend on our ability to listen to our body. Professor Nancy Mangano Rowe, Ph.D., Authentic Movement instructor and author of *Listening Through the Body* writes, "It is through the rich language of my body that I make a connection to my personal truth, my creativity, and my Spirit." She advocates a "checking in" process in which we stop, breathe, pay attention, and then ask for feedback when we are making decisions or searching for solutions. Nancy encourages us to check in with our body, and ask ourselves, "Does my body respond with a thud or a ping?"

A ping is your body saying "yes." The key is to pay attention to the subtle cues. Your body is your best friend and your most reliable and trustworthy ally—trust that it is trying to help you. Not only is your body giving you a constant stream of information to make good decisions, it is also helping you stay strong and healthy. When your body says "yes," you will feel a subtle expansion, a comfortable, gentle release inside you, usually in your chest or abdomen, and sometimes in other areas of your body such as your neck, shoulders, or legs. On the other hand, when your body is telling you "no," you will feel a subtle tightening in your body, a contraction, a sense of holding back. "Yes" feels expansive. "No" feels constrictive. It may take time and practice to tell the difference between your body's yes and no, but once you've got it, this skill will help you for the rest of your life.

Women have fabulous powers of insight and intuition.

However, it can be difficult, if not impossible, to listen skillfully to our senses if we feel disconnected from our body. Many of us have emotionally cut ourselves off from parts of our body—often at the waist or the neck (common places where women feel frozen or disempowered), or where we have experienced trauma. This is no fault of our own. Becoming disconnected from our body is a process that happens over the course of many years, and usually we do not even realize that we are disconnected from parts of ourselves. It may happen as a result of sexual abuse, but it can also be caused by cultural and religious beliefs about the sinful nature of the body—and the sinful nature of the female body in particular. We are given messages as little girls, and then as grown women, to ignore the wisdom we receive from our own body. Over time, we internalize these messages and learn to inhibit ourselves—our feelings, our movements, our natural expressions—in order to win approval, acceptance, and love.

When we become divorced from our body we lose touch with our feminine intelligence, and the pleasure that is part of being a woman. We become disconnected from our natural feminine intuition. Our emotions get stuck inside us, and we lose our connection to the larger life force that flows through us. This is not how nature intended things to be for women. We were born into these fluid bodies to experience everything with our senses—to taste, touch, smell, feel, hear, and intuitively perceive the world around us.

Women have fabulous powers of insight and intuition. Every woman has at least one story—if not many—about feeling a sixth sense. This is especially true for mothers who just seem to know when their child is in trouble or needs help. We know what we know, not only in our mind and our heart, but in our body as well—we get that tight feeling in our stomach, a sudden urge to run, our skin tingles, our breath changes, and our hair stands on end. We may not be able to explain it logically, but we feel it deep within us. The gut feelings we have are our primitive brain talking, giving us information so we can better navigate through life.

A lifetime of cultural conditioning has taught us to ignore, repress, and deny the wisdom that comes from our body. But we can overcome this. We can learn to embrace the knowledge that our female body has to share. First, we must believe that our body is not *less than* the mind or the soul. Our body and soul are made of the same essence. Body movements, sensations, perceptions, and memories are sacred experiences - joyful, pleasurable, full of presence, a gift of life. We must trust that our body knows what to do; it is a source of wisdom, power, and beauty with its own rhythms, seasons, and subtleties.

The body is a sensitive instrument

The human body is a barometer of well-being that feels it's way to knowing what is true, and what is good for us. When we have physical pain, it alerts us to a problem in our body, and when something is not right for us we feel it in our heart, or our gut, or our bones. When we choose to ignore the physical and emotional signals our body sends, we always pay a price. Sometimes we learn the hard way when we go against our gut feelings. But if we understand that our body is sacred, then we can trust the messages that come to us from this exquisite vessel that houses our soul. We need to learn to tune into our body and listen to it, rather than tuning it out and ignoring what it has to say. Gifted mystics and great teachers throughout time have taught that the body and soul are deeply entwined.

The body is always talking to us. It sends us messages through our blood and our bones, through our fingers and toes, through our joints and our tendons, through our soft tender skin, and through all of our senses. In *Women's Bodies, Women's Wisdom* (a must-read for every woman), Dr. Christiane Northrup, M.D. explains how our thoughts, emotions, and brain communicate directly with our immune, nervous, and endocrine systems, and with every organ in our body. The "mind" expands to include every cell of the body, and this creates a sophisticated network of inner guidance, whereby we know things with our body and our brain. Northrup writes, "To be healthy and whole, you must have enough courage to be in touch with the wisdom of your female body, and to follow the desires of your heart."

As we learn to listen deeply to our body,
we will find that it is our teacher, guide, and friend.

If we have experienced things in our life that have caused us to shut down or turn away from this inner guidance system, we can reclaim it. We can learn to tune into the intimate connections between our thoughts, emotions, and physical body. As we learn to listen deeply to our body, we will find that it is our teacher, guide, and friend.

Several years ago, when I was taking a graduate course about the psychology of the body, I had to complete an assignment that included a meditation practice of the body. Deadlines, kids, a neglected husband, and a messy house were all waiting in line for a piece of me. I was feeling impatient, and I needed to get the work done, fast. At last I sat down and started listening to the audio recording. The soothing voice of the instructor gently encouraged me to touch each part of my body and listen while giving it love and appreciation. I started with my feet and worked my way up. I felt nothing, I heard nothing, and I was restless.

The deadline for the assignment was closing in, and I had no choice but to give it another try. This time around I discovered how to have a conversation with my body. My feet began the conversation. They told me that when they are sore and tired they would sincerely appreciate it if I would stop running around like a crazy chicken and put them up for a few minutes. I come from a German family that has a strong work ethic. We are the poster family for working hard and playing hard, and we only stop when we are close to dying. The mere idea of putting my feet up to rest when there are chores to be done feels like sacrilege. While a strong work ethic has served me well, I had not been listening very well to my body. I also realized that when I do not listen to my feet I inevitably develop plantar fasciitis. Through my conversation with my feet, I understood that I have two choices when they hurt. I can power through the pain and limp everywhere until it becomes unbearable, or I can heed the message, slow down, and rest.

We do not have to be suffering from an injury, or in desperate pain, to seek out healing for the body. Sometimes we need help to access the frozen places inside of us. Some women find themselves softly weeping while lying on a massage table. The massage suddenly frees up something buried deep inside them. Massage is just one healing modality. There are many more mind/body therapies that can help heal the body. Some women find that dancing, running, yoga, swimming, biking, or even going for walks is extremely helpful. Afterwards, it feels like something has been lifted, or purged from our body. We are light and free and clear-minded. Building simple practices such as these into our everyday life takes commitment, but the benefits are enormous to our long-term health and well-being.

Emotions get stuck in the body and cause dis-ease

One of the most important lessons we can learn is that when emotions are not acknowledged and expressed they get stuck in the body. Emotions are not supposed to be dammed up—they are supposed to flow through us. We need a full range of emotional expression to be healthy. If we try to deny, numb, ignore, and repress our emotions, they will come out in some unforeseen, and often unfortunate, way.

Dr. Mona Lisa Schulz, M.D., a medical intuitive with a doctorate in behavioral neuroscience and author of *Awakening Intuition: Using Your Mind-Body Network for Insight and Healing* (another must-read for women), uses the framework of the chakras—or emotional centers—to explain how particular imbalances in our body are created by specific emotional patterns. Her work helps us understand that the symptoms we experience in our body are influenced by our emotional life. Our thoughts, feelings, and beliefs directly affect the health of our tissues and organs. There is

Julie Gohman, Ph.D.

a network between our mind, body and emotions that create a unique blueprint of health and dis-ease for each one of us. Each emotional center in our body has corresponding powers and vulnerabilities. Every woman is strong in some emotional centers and weak in others.

Every symptom, illness, and dis-ease that we experience is our body's way of communicating with us.

When we experience physical symptoms or even a life-threatening illness, we can dig deep to discover what the underlying emotional issues are that are manifesting in our body. For example, a woman who didn't start out with a strong sense of safety and security in her childhood is likely to experience symptoms in her first emotional center. This affects the health of the blood, bones, and immune system. A woman who has trouble maintaining her own sense of individual identity within a relationship will tend to have issues in the second emotional center. This is located in the pelvis and affects the lower gastrointestinal tract, bladder, urinary tract, lower back, and reproductive organs.

A woman who feels trapped, stuck, or experiences chronic anxiety will be susceptible to developing issues in the third emotional center, like ulcers and other GI problems. If a woman has trouble expressing all her emotions (especially anger), and feels torn between nurturing others and following her own passions, she is more likely to experience health problems in her fourth emotional center. This is related to heart disease, stroke, and breast cancer. Dr. Mona Lisa teaches that every symptom, illness, and dis-ease that we experience is our body's way of communicating with us that something is out of balance. As we begin to make connections between our emotional patterns and what's happening in our body, we can use this information to make changes that nourish our health and well-being.

If you want to learn more about your emotional patterns, one of the first things you must do is explore the legacy from your childhood. Look back and see how and where your emotional patterns began. For better or worse, your childhood sets the stage for how you perceive the world and your place in it. How you see yourself, how you shape your relationships, and even your patterns of illness or health, begin in your childhood.

Our families teach us how to set boundaries, how to deal with challenges, and how to love and be loved. If no one taught us how to fully express our emotions when we were little, then it is part of our healing journey to do that now. Being able to name how we feel is essential for self-awareness, growth, and healing. We can start naming how we feel by simply stepping back and observing our emotions—without judging them or ourselves for having them. We can witness them like we would watch the traffic from a distance. We can say, "There goes some anger. Now, some fear. Finally, some sadness." Nothing is held back, suppressed, or denied.

When we stop denying our emotions, we are ready to explore how our emotional patterns are affecting our life. And when we understand this, we can let go of the patterns that are not serving our health and happiness. Consider it a matter of life and death. By attending to our emotional life, we in turn, are attending to our health. By consciously releasing emotional patterns that are not good for us, we can create healthier ways of being that have a positive affect on our body.

No matter what age we are, it is possible to learn to accept and express all our emotions. We need to understand that we do not have to wait for someone to give us permission to feel our anger, pain, disappointment, or sadness. And most importantly, we need to stop berating ourselves for how we feel. What we feel is what we feel, and no matter what it is, it is okay. In fact, it is necessary to feel what we feel if we want to prevent our emotions from lodging in us and causing dis-ease. Every woman, through her own process of self-discovery, can find her way to emotional well-being and wholeness.

Reconnecting with a larger life force in nature

An important part of listening to our body includes rediscovering the connection we have to the larger life force that exists within and around everyone and everything. Spending time in nature reminds us that the Earth is our mother. It reconnects our body to the ground that we stand on. As we drink in the raw beauty of nature we are filled with calm, and we rediscover the web of relationships that connect everything. We remember that our human world is entwined with other worlds, and with many layers of life we cannot see. When we are in nature, our body enters into a silent conversation and mysterious union with the natural world. Nature has a marvelous ability to soften our heart, quiet our mind, and restore a feeling of deep gladness for life.

Whether we are walking through a forest, swimming in the ocean, or climbing up a mountain the plants, animals, and clean air and water have the power to rejuvenate us like nothing else. As we feel the sun on our face, watch the birds soar through the sky, and feel the earth beneath our feet, nature heals us.

Spending time in nature is also an opportunity to discover the peace and beauty that exists within us. The more we see the natural beauty around us, the more we can recognize the natural beauty inside us. For example, when we are in a park or a forest we can settle into the grass and look up at the trees and into the canopy. We notice that the trees have dark knots and scars, strong limbs, and rough patches of bark. They have branches that move and bend, and sometimes break. Some trees are planted in rich, fertile soil. Some trees are in the desert sand. And some trees grow and thrive despite harsh and rocky conditions. And yet, if you look closely, every tree has its own beauty—just like us.

When we find special places on this Earth that feel like home, we come home to our body. Gratitude always wells up within me when I spend time in water, the place where I feel most connected to the divine. My soul is saying, "Thank you for bringing me home." I feel a huge wave of relief roll over me as peace fills my body. In this beauty and silence of nature, my wholeness is restored. Ask yourself where you feel completely relaxed. Where can you let go of all your worries and breathe deeply? When does the mental chatter stop for you? Where on this earth do you feel most at home?

When we find special places on this Earth that feel like home, we come home to our body.

Sometimes when we least expect it, we find answers to our questions and messages for our soul. It may be in the quiet of a forest or on the waves of the sea. Many years ago, while visiting a sequoia grove in California—a magical and enchanting otherworld—I came across this advice from a tree (and I have kept it taped to my desk ever since):

> *Stand tall and proud*
> *Sink your roots into the Earth*
> *Be content with your natural beauty*
> *Go out on a limb*
> *Drink plenty of water*
> *Remember your roots*
> *Enjoy the view*

Everything in the natural world can help us shift from our crazy, frantic pace of life to one that is slower, more peaceful, where we can become deeply attuned to the wisdom of our body. We all need time in nature, and times of solitude and silence, to come home to our body and to refresh our soul. Whether it is a well-planned camping trip in the wilderness or a stroll through the flowers in a nearby park, we can each find a way to reconnect with the earth. Nature gives us a gift that is so hard to come by in our modern world—a chance to just…be.

Learning to listen to your body

You can learn to listen to your body. You can reclaim your natural feminine intelligence and use your inner guidance system to make authentic life choices that lead to health, happiness, and harmony in your body, mind, and spirit.

There are some basic things we can do to get in touch with, and honor, the sacred vessel we inhabit. Eight practices follow: mirror work, tuning into our body, eating well, asking ourselves what we are really hungry for, moving our body, enjoying nature, making the link between symptoms and emotions, and getting a massage or some other form of bodywork. Explore the practices that appeal to you and give them a try. Commit to showing love to your whole body every day.

Mirror work

Each morning or night, sit or stand in front of a mirror and thank your body for all it has done for you. Say positive affirmations, and send it love. Acknowledge your natural state as radiant health and joy. When you love your body, you will naturally want to care for it very well.

Tune into your body

When you have a decision to make, sit quietly with your body and tune into your breathing, heart rate, and sensations. What do you notice? Is there a pit in your stomach? Does your whole body tighten up? Does your body relax? What happens to your breathing? These are clues to help guide you. Listen.

Eat well

You are what you eat. When you make healthy food choices—like fruits and vegetables instead of chips and cookies—your body will be a clearer, lighter, and happier vessel. Stock your cupboards with whole foods that are healthy. Start your day with a good breakfast, and pack simple snacks such as apples and raw almonds for when you are busy and on the go.

Julie Gohman, Ph.D.

What are you *really* hungry for?

When you find yourself craving sweets, or mashed potatoes, or something that comforts you, ask yourself: what am I *really* hungry for? Sometimes our body is deficient in certain nutrients and therefore we crave certain foods, but sometimes we are unconsciously craving more "sweetness" in life and using food to fill the void.

Move your body

Create a regular exercise routine doing something you enjoy—running, swimming, dancing, walking, biking, yoga, Pilates, or whatever feels good to your body. Make a commitment to move your body every day. Stretch yourself, try new activities, join a group, get up early, and listen to your body for feedback.

Enjoy nature

Spend time in nature. We are living bodies in a living world. When we spend time close to the Earth, we lose the chatter and noise of daily life, and we gain the freedom and joy of simply being present to the natural beauty that is all around us.

Make the link between symptoms and emotions

If you get headaches, stiff neck and shoulders, or are frequently sick, try to pinpoint the emotional situations that trigger the symptoms. The symptoms are messages from the body trying to get our attention about something in our life that needs to change.

Get a massage or bodywork

Get a massage, or find a skilled practitioner in some other system of bodywork that appeals to you. Explore the wide variety of options that are available. Consider the money you spend on these services as part of what keeps you happy, healthy and balanced.

As you begin listening to your body, consider the words of Martha Graham, who said, "The body is a sacred garment. It's your first and last garment; it is what you enter life in and what you depart life with, and it should be treated with honor." It is time to begin cherishing your human body, and listening to its wisdom, for it is the place that your spirit calls "home" in this world.

The question to ask yourself is:
What is my body trying to tell me?

Julie Gohman, Ph.D.

For your sacred temple

*May you be blessed
with the inner spark
to nourish your essence
with senses wide open.*

*May you listen deeply
to the intelligence
of your amazing body
a source of guidance and wisdom.*

*May you honor
every emotion that flows
through your being
as a message of love.*

*May you live
ever faithful, ever grateful
to the sacred temple
that illuminates your soul.*

The Seventh Sacred Question

What is my body trying to tell me?

Julie Gohman, Ph.D.

What is my body trying to tell me?

The Eighth Sacred Question

Am I Ready To Dance With The Moon?

> *Does it come as a surprise that I dance like I have got diamonds at the meeting of my thighs?*
> —Maya Angelou

Thousands of years ago, ancient peoples looked up to the sky and watched the moon. They recognized its cyclical rhythm, and they made the connection between the moon's phases and the cycles in human life. There was a sacred wholeness that infused everything that existed.

Women in these cultures identified with the Moon Mother. The feminine image was sacred and divine, and women danced under the light of the full moon for rituals and celebrations. The Great Creator was not imagined as a man sitting on a throne up in the heavens, but as a Creatress, a woman—earthy, sensual, powerful, and nourishing. She was known by many names, including the Moon Goddess, the Great Goddess, and the Great Mother of the Universe.

Women were not considered to be the weaker sex in these times, but were immensely respected and revered.

Julie Gohman, Ph.D.

We were considered to have earthly and divine powers. The mysteries of the female body and childbirth took on sacred dimensions that represented the mystery of life itself. Images of the female body took on religious significance. For example, the flowing breast of a mother was the symbol of trust in the universe for nourishment. The shape of a triangle was the symbol for a woman's vulva, the divine threshold through which life emerges. Statues, paintings, and images of the Mother Goddess adorned every home as a sign of the organic, sacred life force, an energy that infused everything. This deep reverence for the feminine can be traced back through time to the very beginning. It seems humanity's first image of life was a mother.

Scholars have discovered from ancient texts that the mother in every Babylonian house was known as the "goddess of the house." Every woman's home was a temple, and she was the living goddess. According to *The Women's Encyclopedia of Myths and Secrets* by Barbara Walker, property in ancient Greece was called "temenos," meaning "land belonging to the moon"—or land belonging to women. In fact, almost all ancient societies were matriarchal. Women owned the land, governed the communities, and chose their husbands. Inheritances were handed down from mother to daughter. This is why the ancient Greek heroes had to leave home to seek their fortunes—their sisters got it all.

These human goddesses were strong, industrious, and prosperous. They viewed themselves with love, not disdain. They embraced their thighs, their age, and each other with grace, kindness, and harmony. They caressed each other's beautiful pregnant bellies and helped each other when it was time to give birth. They drew their young girls close and initiated them into the mysteries of womanhood. Old women were not cast aside. They were honored for their wisdom and experience. These women were passionate and fierce mothers, daughters, sisters, and lovers of the world.

The eternal promise of the moon

Karen Armstrong, the world-renowned religious scholar, teaches that ancient peoples saw the divine in everything. They celebrated the rhythms of life and the rhythms of the moon, and embraced its eternal promise of renewal—darkness is always followed by light.

Tales of the moon are found all over the world. Cultures everywhere saw the moon as the eternal "Great Mother." The Sioux Indians called the moon "The Old Woman Who Never Dies." In South America, Peruvians named the moon "Mama Quilla," and "Mama Ogllo." She was both mother and daughter. The Persians looked at the moon and called her "Metra," meaning "mother, whose love penetrated everywhere." The Egyptians considered the moon to be the "Mother of the Universe." The Polynesians believed in a "Creatress Hina," meaning the moon. The moon was the first woman and the image for every woman thereafter. In a similar fashion, the Finns called their Creatress "Luonnotar," meaning "Luna, the Moon." Scandinavians called their Creatress "Mardoll," meaning "Moon Shining Over the Sea." In Germany, people worshipped the moon as "Heva" (Eve). She was the "Mother of All Living." Britain was once called Albion, which means "The Milk-white Moon-goddess." And in other parts of Europe the Moon Goddess was called "Our Lady" and "Mother of God."

The lunar cycle became intertwined with the cycles and stages of womanhood. Menstruation is often referred to as "moon time." And the four phases of the moon were known to have magical energies that marked the stages of birth, growth, decay, and death and regeneration. Each phase has specific meaning for women.

The waxing moon is like a blooming young maiden. The energy of the waxing moon is about growth, learning, building, and being creative. During this phase, you may find yourself thinking about what you want to increase in your life, and what you want to draw to you—a new job, a new home, a new love. Spring is the season that matches the energy of the waxing moon. There are little buds on tree branches, flowers that begin to open, and the sowing of seeds in the rich soil of the Earth.

The full moon represents fertility and motherhood—times when a woman is "full" of life. The energy of the full moon relates to abundance, the manifestation of desires, achieving dreams, and sexuality. The full moon casts a vibe that is exuberant, celebratory, and exhilarating. This is when you will feel like taking action towards something you have dreamed of or longed for. Summer is the season that parallels the energy of the full moon. The buds on the tree branches are uncurled, the flowers are large and lush, and the plants in the garden are flourishing.

The waning moon is like a wise old woman; her light shines from within. The energy of the waning moon is about shedding old ways, letting go, cleansing, releasing, and making space. You may decide to eliminate negative people from your life, or transition out of a job you no longer enjoy. This is a time to get rid of things, declutter, and unburden your life. Autumn is the season that corresponds to the energy of the waning moon. The trees are shedding their leaves, the flowers are beginning to wither and die, and it is time to reap the bounty of the garden.

The dark moon comes when the moon is in the Earth's shadow; it is invisible to the naked eye—like a child forming in the womb of a woman. We cannot see the light although we know it is there, and so we learn to wait and trust. The energy of the dark moon is about resting, finding peace, and listening to the longings of your soul—it is a time of renewal and stillness. It has been compared to a cocoon holding a butterfly. During the dark moon, you might feel tired or crave quiet solitude. Winter is the season that resembles the energy of the dark moon. The trees appear barren; the flowers are no longer blooming, and the seeds in the garden are dormant.

After three days, the crescent moon reappears in the sky as the wondrous sign of new beginnings. A sliver of light, the new moon brings optimism and hope. Anne Baring and Jules Cashford, authors of *The Myth of the Goddess* said, "Moon, woman, earth—and the cycle of gestation in all three—can be seen to be governed by rhythm, order, and an exact sequence of development." Since the beginning of time, the orbit of the moon, like the monthly round of a woman's cycle, has evoked people to see the mysterious patterns where the invisible becomes visible, and where the shadows give way to the light.

The wisdom of the moon

The moon and its mythical powers have fascinated people throughout the ages, and the moon has become a powerful symbol woven into language. Today we understand "moonstruck" as being in love. Being "over the moon" is a state of great joy or happiness. And to "shoot for the moon" means to be very ambitious.

Native Americans use different names for the moon throughout the year. They call it "wolf moon" in January, and "flower moon" in May. In June, it is the "strawberry moon," and in September—a time when trees are full of juicy, ripe fruit—it is known as "red plum moon." By November, it is the "frosty moon," and in December it is aptly named "long nights moon." These names connect the changing seasons on Earth to the constant of a celestial body.

The many Native American names for the moon express a wisdom that can be found in all spiritual traditions. It is the wisdom and power in naming and claiming what is active and alive in the present moment. The delicious, juicy moments of life, and the cold and bleak moments of life both deserve acknowledgement. The phases of the moon represent just about everything we can experience. Whether you are experiencing great joy and satisfaction right now or deep despair and darkness, know that all of your emotions and experiences deserve to be named and claimed. Think of it like the phases of the moon, there is no shame in saying that sometimes the moon is hidden in darkness, and sometimes it is shining brightly in the sky.

All of your emotions and experiences deserve to be named and claimed.

Although many superstitious beliefs about the moon have changed, we cannot deny its effects. Its gravitational pull affects the changing ocean tides, and this same pull is felt in our human body. Studies have shown that the moon influences women's menstrual cycles. Sexual desire, ovulation and conception tends to peak when the moon is full. And it is during the new moon that many women start their menstrual bleeding. From the onset of the menstrual cycle until ovulation feelings of optimism pervade. Women are more likely to have new ideas, and start creative projects. Midcycle is when we often become receptive to others. Our bodies secret pheromones that increase our sexual attractiveness; this is when we are most fertile. After ovulation, in the luteal phase, women enter a time that is more reflective in nature. We tend to evaluate difficult aspects of our lives that need to be changed or adjusted. Sometimes we need more time alone as we draw inward. Each phase of our cycle affects our dreams, our energy, and our creativity.

*Sometimes we feel sexy and wild,
sometimes we feel lazy or grumpy or both.*

We can see that our menstrual cycle also reflects the cyclical nature of our moods and emotions and the swells and dips in our relationships. Sometimes we cry, sometimes we laugh. Sometimes we make a friend, sometimes we lose a friend. Sometimes we feel sexy and wild, sometimes we feel lazy or grumpy or both. Sometimes we rant, sometimes we are quiet. Sometimes we scream and fight, sometimes we make peace. Sometimes we feel on top of the world, and sometimes we feel lost and alone.

Like the cycle of the moon, every woman has her natural rhythms. All of these times are part of the ebb and flow of a woman's journey. Whether things are expanding or contracting, whether it is a time of rest or upheaval, or a time of joy or sadness, these are all part and parcel of life. Rather than struggling against these things, we can greet them as a knock at the door that brings an invitation to love and accept our divine feminine nature.

The wisdom of the moon empowers us to name and claim what is active and alive in us in the present moment, whatever it is—knowing that the darkness is always followed by light. We can embrace our sowing and our reaping, our lovemaking and our fighting, our joy and our sorrow, knowing that one will turn into the other and that each is part of the whole.

Moon blood

Menstrual blood was sometimes called "moon blood." Most of us do not realize that it was considered magical until fairly recently. Early creation myths tell us that man was made from "clay and moon blood." Chinese sages considered menstrual blood to be the essence of Mother Earth that gives life to all things. In Taoism, women's menstrual blood was called "red yin juice" that came from a woman's "Mysterious Gateway." Ancient Greeks called menstrual blood "supernatural red wine" which the gods depended on because of its miraculous power. They believed the wisdom of both men and gods was in their blood because of the soul-stuff given to them by their mothers. In Christianity, the blood in a woman's uterus was considered the "moonflower" that contains the soul of future generations. In Persia, menstrual blood was a sacred elixir of immortality called "the milk of mother Goddess."

Many women have been taught to see the natural cycles we go through as embarrassing, dirty, and shameful. Rather than welcoming the rhythms of womanhood, we are conditioned to dread and fear them. And we are taught that if we cannot resist these things outright, then we must at least do our best to conceal or fight against them. So we dutifully hide our menstruation, repress our sexuality, numb our childbirth, and fight the aging process.

I was blessed with a mother who taught me about menstruation without calling it a curse. She showed me how to care for myself tenderly, telling me to take a hot bath and rest. Despite this lovely introduction, I did not consider my blood to be sacred until I learned about ancient cultures that honored the feminine. Suddenly, I saw my menstrual cycle in a whole new light. Instead of popping Advil and powering through my days, I slowed down and listened to my body. I rested more and did less. I gave my body the tender loving care it deserved. Menstruation was no longer just a messy inconvenience; it was a monthly opportunity to honor the life-giving substance of my womb.

The color red was and continues to be, a sacred color all over the world because of its association with women, blood, sexual potency, and creative power. The fabled fountain of eternal youth was said to overflow once every lunar month, and it was clearly related to the menstrual blood of women. Easter eggs were classic womb-symbols of the Goddess Eostre; they were traditionally colored red and put on graves. And Australian Aborigines painted their sacred objects and their bodies with red ochre for religious ceremonies—symbolizing women's menstrual blood—which they linked to the process of rebirth.

I recently had the pleasure of attending the screening of the groundbreaking documentary called *Things We Do Not Talk About: Women's Stories From The Red Tent* by young filmmaker Isadora Gabrielle Leidenfrost. The film is about the Red Tent Temple Movement—inspired by Anita Diamant's 1997 book *The Red Tent*. There is a movement happening all over the world to create "Red Tent" spaces for women of all ages and all cycles. The vision of the movement is to create close, sustaining, and strong communities of women. The movement's website (redtenttemplemovement.com) notes: "The Red Tent Temple Movement raises up a Red Tent in our local villages, cities and towns for us to honor our blood cycles and womanhood journeys." The Red Tent offers women a place where they can slow down and just be. In the film, Leidenfrost captures the experiences of women who gathered together under a red tent to rest, share their stories, dance, eat, cry, laugh, and support one another. In these safe places where only women go, open conversations about taboo subjects flourish. Women relax knowing other women who understand their joys and sorrows surround them. They emerge from the red tent replenished, feeling the strength that comes when women gather together.

Whether we are still menstruating or not, we can appreciate the incredible beauty and power of our womanly body and our moon blood. We are sacred and creative creatures—the power of the divine feminine is within us.

Dancing with the moon

Dancing, in all parts of the world, has traditionally been part of festivals and celebrations. The joy of music and laughter and togetherness affirms the goodness of life. The power of dance is how deeply it moves us on every level of our being—mind, body, and spirit. Throughout time, women have danced, by themselves and with others, to express the beauty of the feminine, and the sacredness of life.

Dancing means to move in rhythm—often in unity with others—and preferably with passion. It is an act of moving with, and not against, the natural urges and rhythms of our body. As we reconnect with our divine feminine nature, through dancing or in some other way that suits us, we free the longings of our soul that ache to come alive. In ancient times, women embraced their femininity as a spiritual path, and we can too, with a little inspiration from our sisters of long ago.

Imagine yourselves on a midsummer's night. You are wearing a crown of ivy and flowers in your long hair that is flowing down your back in wild tangles. It's a warm evening, and it feels good to be out under the stars and the moon. You are dancing around in a circle with a group of women. Your bonds to each other, as mothers, daughters, sisters, and friends are a source of great joy, and it makes you smile as you look around at these beautiful women. In the glow of the moonlight, you can see their round hips, soft bellies, and generous breasts that have fed many children.

*How good it is to be alive,
and how fortunate it is to be a woman.*

You feel the pulse of life coursing through your veins, reminding you of the sacredness of womanhood. You think about how good it is to be alive, and how fortunate it is to be a woman. This is the "Dance of Life," where women's power, bodies, and bonds of sisterhood are celebrated and honored for their strength and beauty.

Dancing with the moon is a celebration of the natural rhythms of womanhood. If we had lived thousands of years ago it would have been normal to dance under the light of a full moon. We would have known that our sexuality is sacred, our body is powerful, and our moon blood is the magical substance that gives life. We would have known that all women are goddesses.

Julie Gohman, Ph.D.

We are all moon goddesses

Thinking about your womanhood with reverence allows something inside of you to begin healing. You will feel the bonds of connection to the moon, the stars, the ocean, the trees, the animals, and especially other women. You will fall in love with the sacredness of your body, the sacredness of the Earth, and the sacredness of life itself.

Goddess energy brings four gifts to every woman, according to Carol P. Christ, Ph.D., author of *Why Women Need the Goddess*. The first gift is that the Goddess is a symbol of our female power. Women are strong, creative, and independent human beings, and there is no reason to play small or bow down as the weaker sex, ever.

The second gift is that the Goddess affirms the inherent beauty and goodness of our female body. Yes, we menstruate, give birth, and nourish our babies with milk from our breasts—we are earthy, and fleshy, and full of the blood that gives life to this world. There is nothing dirty or wrong with our female bodily functions. Our natural cycles of womanhood are something to celebrate.

The third gift is that the Goddess affirms a woman's will, which means every woman is responsible for defining who she is and what she wants. Our culture often gives women the message that they should be subordinate and wait for others to take the initiative, but the Goddess does not agree. She encourages women to believe in themselves. She says to us, "be assertive, and use your talents in positive, life-giving ways."

Lastly, the energy of the Goddess says to us—look to your bonds with other women as a precious and sacred part of life. Our bonds to each other, as mothers and daughters, sisters, friends, colleagues, and lovers are worth fighting for—celebrate them, honor them, and place them in a position of importance.

When the goddess emerges in you, you will naturally become more loving to yourself because you treasure your womanhood. Perhaps you will begin watching the moon closely, and notice how your monthly rhythms are aligned with the cycles in nature. As you look up into the sky and see how she goes through her lunar cycle, you will be reminded to gently embrace the changes in your life. Every season and every phase is an important part of womanhood. The moon will quietly awaken in your heart the desire to honor your own feminine journey.

*Look to your bonds with other women
as a precious and sacred part of life.*

Just as the crescent moon is the beginning of a new lunar cycle, you too can feel new beginnings stirring—it may be an idea, a relationship, a new life. You may have a desire to travel to places you've never been, discover new things about yourself, or nourish a passion that is growing in you. The full moon stage of womanhood is a time of nurturance—an opportunity to see how you are a powerful channel of maternal compassion, a bounty of love that is supreme. As you are busy sharing that bounty of love with others remember to offer your true self some of it too. Nourish your body, your mind, and your spirit so you can stay strong and full of life. When the moon begins to wane, just as we will someday, you can continue shining your light every day, knowing that each stage of life has its beauty and joy. The waning moon is also telling you to let go of whatever is no longer alive—toxic relationships, unhealthy situations, dead-end jobs—only you can know what it is that needs to die away. Eventually, darkness comes to us all, and that too is something we can embrace instead of fear.

*Trust yourself and your feminine intuition
through all the phases of womanhood.*

You are a glorious goddess, and you are on a spiritual journey. Trust yourself and your feminine intuition through all the phases of womanhood—the young girl you once were, the beautiful woman you are now, and the wise old woman you are becoming. Acknowledging your goddess nature means embracing the innocent years of being a child, the nurturing years of being a mother, the wisdom years of growing older, and the darkness that finally comes to gather you. As Starhawk writes of the Goddess: "She is death as well as birth, dark as well as light."

Ancient peoples knew that when the moon disappeared for three days it would always reappear. Where the moon went was a mystery, just as it is still a mystery where we will go, but we must remember the eternal promise of the moon—the darkness is always followed by light. Knowing this gave ancient peoples and can give us, a sense of harmony and peace about the ultimate rhythm of all things.

*The question to ask yourself is:
Am I ready to dance with the moon?*

For The Goddess In You

May you be blessed
with the joy of a young girl
the excitement of new beginnings
and an unquenchable curiosity.

May you be blessed
with the spirit of adventure
and hold nothing back
as you grow into a strong woman.

May you be blessed
with dreams come true
as you nurture the world
with a mother's love.

May you be blessed
as the light of your soul
burns brightly from within
and you become a wise old woman.

May you be blessed
with a peaceful heart
when death walks by your side
that you may look back on your life
and be glad you danced with the moon.

Julie Gohman, Ph.D.

Am I ready to dance with the moon?

The Eighth Sacred Question

Am I ready to dance with the moon?

The Ninth Sacred Question

How Can I Fill My Life With Ecstasy?

*The soul should always stand ajar,
ready to welcome the ecstatic experience.*
—Emily Dickinson

Most of us think about sex, drugs, or altered states of consciousness when we hear the word ecstasy. But ecstasy is far greater than any of these things. It is more than just feeling good or having fun. When we experience ecstasy we are touching the timeless and eternal; we are experiencing the divine. And experiencing the divine is blissful. It is the welling up of energy of something beyond ourselves. Ecstasy brings the energy of transcendent wisdom and mystery.

Bliss and ecstatic experiences bring deep states of joy, peace, gratitude, and awe. They build up like waves on the ocean before they crash over the shore of our soul. Ecstasy allows us to transcend life as we know it, to touch something that is beyond us. Moments such as these eventually slip from our grasp and fade away. But once we open ourselves to ecstasy it is never far away, and we can experience it again and again.

Our body is made for ecstasy. We come alive when we allow the physical pathways of our body to receive pleasure. When we live with our senses wide open, the intelligence of our body leads us towards experiences that feel good. When we experience a hearty belly laugh, a soft kiss, a bite of delicious food, the perfume of spring blossoms, or a moving piece of music something frees up inside of us. Our senses are showing us how to live more fully and deeply. When we allow ecstasy to flow through us, our whole body and soul glows with the pleasure of being alive. Life becomes one sweet moment after another.

*Ecstasy is about surrendering ourselves
to the passion of the present,
the bliss of now.*

Ecstasy is available to every woman. However, many of us have a hard time embracing life as an ecstatic experience. What does it even mean to live in ecstasy? Living an ecstatic life is not about seeking constant bliss, or avoiding the difficult or upsetting things that happen. Ecstasy is about surrendering ourselves to the passion of the present, the bliss of now. The nature of ecstasy is to show us fleeting glimpses of the eternal in simple moments of pleasure.

Opening to ecstasy through laughter

Many women are cut off from an ecstatic life because they have become disconnected from their body, and therefore the natural pathways of pleasure are inhibited. But there is a simple, easy, and cheap way to rediscover pleasure—it is to begin laughing more. Laughter is a wonderful way to reconnect with the power of ecstasy because it works on every level of our being—mind, body, and spirit. We were born to laugh; consider how easily babies smile and giggle. Even if we did not grow up in a household where laughter was a common sound, we can learn to laugh now.

Laughter awakens our body and our emotions. It is a physical, elemental, and vitalizing experience. Laughing triggers the release of endorphins in our body, a key factor to feeling good. Our respiration and circulation improve, and we tone muscles while we are laughing. A good, hearty laugh reduces stress and tension, and our body experiences a deep relaxation response. Laughter increases immune cells and antibodies, thus improving our resistance to disease. When we laugh, our outlook brightens. Our thinking improves, and creativity surges. In short, nothing works faster or more dependably to bring our mind and body back into balance than a good laugh. Laughing is an easy to use practice that lightens our burdens, keeps us grounded, and brings us pleasure.

A good belly laugh is like making love;
it creates ripples of pleasure throughout our body.

Laughter can also be very sensual. A good belly laugh is like making love; it creates ripples of pleasure throughout our body. Like an orgasm, our whole body is swept into a rhythmic response of joy. When we laugh with the ones that we love, our bonds of intimacy are strengthened. There is unity in laughter (as long as it is not at someone's expense).

Having a sense of humor and being playful helps keep things fresh and exciting. We feel more emotionally and physically connected when we giggle and tease and tickle and act silly. One of the simplest things we can do to feel more ecstasy in our life is to infuse all our relationships with a large dose of laughter.

As we learn to find the humor in all our experiences, we become more resilient. When we are going through a difficult time, we need our friends and loved ones to support us, and we also need laughter. Laughter can lift our sadness, shift our perspective, and make us happy to be alive. Khalil Gibran, the Lebanese poet, wrote, "In the sweetness of friendship let there be laughter and sharing of pleasures. For in the dew of little things, the heart finds its morning and is refreshed."

When we cannot stop laughing, something gives way in our soul, and like a dam that overflows, we feel lighter and freer. We breathe easier, and our whole body relaxes. This is sacred laughter. Though we cannot see it happening, we know that something is healing inside us. As we open to ecstasy through laughter, we smile more. We loosen up and stop taking ourselves so seriously. We attract fun, playful people. We find ourselves drawn to laughter wherever we find it, at home, work, with our loved ones, or in a crowd of strangers. And we naturally start dwelling on all the good things in our life, knowing that we have the choice every day—to laugh or not—it's up to us.

Living with joy

There are many life paths you can choose, just as there are many ways you can serve others. So how do you know which life path will bring joy and which will bring struggle? Most of us are so busy fulfilling our daily obligations that we don't even know what it is that makes us feel happy. Do you know? If I asked you what brings joy to your life would you be able to answer?

One of the most important questions about finding joy involves stepping back from the busyness (I know this isn't easy my friend) and asking ourselves if we are waiting for that someday in the future when we will be happy. Are you sacrificing today's joy for an image of what life will be like when everything's better? What about right now? Would you like to create a life that is filled with so much joy that every day becomes a whirlwind of ecstasy? It all begins when we pay attention to our energy.

The vital energy in our body is known as chi in Chinese traditions and prana in yogic traditions. The flow of this subtle energy through the unseen pathways of the body is known as the "subtle body" or the "energy body." We cannot see a person's subtle energy, but we feel it. We each have an energy field that either attracts us to or repels us away from people, places, things, and even ideas. This energy is an essential ingredient in why we feel a certain magnetism for people or places in this world. When we meet someone who is vibrantly alive, someone who oozes joy from their pores, we are drawn to them. We want what they have, and being around them makes us feel good. There is something different and special that we can feel more than we can see.

*When we value who we are,
and listen to the voice that whispers from our soul,
we find ourselves moving in joyful directions.*

We exchange chi, or vital energy, with other human beings all the time. We are exchanging the energy of our aliveness with one another. This happens in intimately situations when we make love face to face, belly to belly, and heart to heart. We also exchange chi in less intimate ways. We greet co-workers, we engage with children, we spend time with family and friends. Having a personal conversation with a close friend can be a deep exchange of both mental and emotional energy. We need this exchange of energy to lift our spirits, connect with someone who cares, and show love in return. To a large degree, how we interact with the people around us is a powerful reflection of this subtle energy we feel. It determines who we feel safe with, and where we feel comfortable. When we value who we are, and listen to the voice that whispers from our soul, we find ourselves moving in joyful directions—towards people and places that bring us up rather than tear us down.

Like a sublime instrument, our body and mind create beautiful music when we feel a strong and powerful flow of vital energy coursing through us. We feel on top of the world. We begin creative projects. We believe in ourselves. Doubt and worry fade away. Positive energy rushes in. There is nothing that feels more invigorating than to be filled with this raw enthusiasm and hope for life. And that is how we know we are on the path of joy.

You have the power to create a joyful life—
love yourself and take the leap.

If all this sounds good, but you are nowhere near an ecstatic experience, understand that ecstasy is relative, and you can take small steps to get there. In Ecstasy is Necessary, Barbara Carrellas writes "It is not a fixed destination in some faraway land, reachable only after you lose weight, clear all your chakras, learn the entire Kama Sutra, spend years in therapy, meditate extensively, study with a guru, and find a better partner." Ecstasy can be found everywhere as you travel along life's pathways. When you wake up tomorrow morning, ask yourself what you could do that would bring joy and delight. And then get quiet and listen. Nothing fancy or complicated is required. You have the power to create a joyful life—love yourself and take the leap.

Mindfulness and ecstasy in the ordinary

When we begin to think about ecstasy, it may seem incongruent with our everyday reality. We cannot just ignore our daily work as a mother, wife, and worker bee. The two-year-old having a tantrum and the kids jumping on the couch need a mother right now. The dishes need to be done, the laundry needs to be washed, there is a job to go to, and the barking dog wants to be walked. Ecstasy seems far, far away from all these things, perhaps in another galaxy.

I have, of course, run into these roadblocks myself. When I first began to think about life as a pleasure-filled experience, it all seemed like a rather tragic paradox. How could I find ecstasy in the overwhelming demands of modern life? I knew that I wanted to feel more happiness, more pleasure—even in the humdrum moments I wanted to feel more alive.

After much searching, I finally found a practice that has helped me find the ecstasy in the ordinary—it is called mindfulness. A few years ago, I was taking a class and had to read several books about mindfulness. One of them was *The Miracle of Mindfulness* by Thích Nhat Hanh—Buddhist monk, teacher, and activist. Another was *Real Happiness* by meditation teacher and author Sharon Salzberg, who explains it this way, "Mindfulness refines our attention so that we can connect fully and directly with whatever life brings."

Mindfulness means being completely present to whatever is before us. It is an energy that helps us enjoy what is happening right now. Mindfulness could be described as paying attention on purpose. We are staying in the present moment, which is one of the hardest things for most people to do. Whatever we are doing, or whomever we are with, becomes most important.

Anyone can practice mindfulness; it is not a religion, and there are no rules you must follow. A simple way to try mindfulness is to close your eyes and breathe. Breath is the bridge that unites our body to our thoughts, and it is key to mindfulness. Breathing can be used to center our mind when it becomes scattered. Taking deep breaths is like calming a choppy lake, transforming it into a surface that is smooth and peaceful. Not only is mindfulness good for our brain, it has also been shown to improve our mood, boost our immune function, decrease stress, and promote healing. It is a practice that can profoundly transform our everyday life.

The beauty of mindfulness is that it quiets our mind and opens our heart so we can experience life as it is unfolding. Mindfulness is practiced in the course of daily life; there is no need to put it off until we have time to be alone, sit on a cushion, and meditate. If we are walking, we can walk as if

Julie Gohman, Ph.D.

we are kissing the earth with our feet, as Thich Nhat Hanh suggests. We can take in our surroundings with all our senses. If we are dealing with a tired and whiney child, we can choose to be fully present and empathize, and not just wish the behavior would stop. When we brush our teeth or wash our face, we feel every motion, every sensation. When we eat a meal, we slow down and pay attention to the flavor and the texture of food, and it becomes a culinary experience. When we are listening to someone, our mind is not formulating a comeback, but completely attuned to what the other person is saying. This is how to live in the moment instead of being stuck in the past or leaping ahead to the future.

> *The beauty of mindfulness is that it*
> *quiets our mind and opens our heart.*

How much ecstasy we feel in everyday life is dependent on how much we are willing to let in. If we aren't living in the present moment, right now, ecstasy will pass us by. It is like having a winning lottery ticket and refusing to cash it in. We miss out on the riches that are waiting for us. When I find myself thinking about something other than what I am actually doing, I try to bring my attention back to the present moment. When I am washing dishes, instead of growing impatient, I try to enjoy the feel of warm water and silky bubbles on my hands. I think about how good it feels to create a clean and harmonious environment to live in. When my children are talking to me, I try to give them my undivided attention. I stop what I am doing, look into their eyes, and focus on what they are saying. Even if they are telling me about the worms in their pocket, it becomes the most important thing for me to hear. I am not always successful; my mind tends to be a monkey, swinging from thought to thought through the jungle of life. I make mistakes, and I begin again. I stray from the path, and I begin again. With the practice of mindfulness, each moment is a new beginning. We continue to get more chances to show up and be present in our own lives. If we are willing – each moment becomes an opportunity to cultivate joy and ecstasy.

Each moment is a new beginning.

Given the frantic pace of modern life, and the distracted way we move through our days, mindfulness can be extremely difficult to put into practice. However, every single situation becomes an opportunity to practice being fully present—including all the mundane, dreary tasks that we face each day. It is not easy to be mindful in everything we do. Mindfulness requires us to slow down—and it takes a commitment on our part to change our ways, but ultimately when we learn to practice mindfulness we rediscover the simple pleasures in everyday moments.

The path to a life of ecstasy

If we want to live an ecstatic life, we must first decide that we are worthy of it. We must believe, as a friend of mine likes to say that when we are feeling good, we are feeling God. We have to trust that being happy and healthy and feeling radiantly alive will allow us to show up as the greatest version of ourselves.

Every woman can find ecstasy in her life, in small moments and simple pleasures. Making little changes such as leisurely sipping our morning coffee or tea, instead of gulping it down as we race out the door, can help us start our day with more awareness. The delight of fluffy bath towels, or soft candlelight can help anchor us in the present. Listening to the purr of a cat, or picking a ripe apple from a tree can become beautiful moments for us. Simple pleasures such as the scent of rain, a cool ocean breeze, or a rainbow in the sky can remind us how magnificent life is. Wherever we live, we can find beauty. Beauty is not something outside of us; it is how we learn to see the world. As we begin enjoying the abundance that is freely given to us, ecstasy will find us everywhere we go.

Beauty is not something outside of us;
it is how we learn to see the world.

Exploring our inner world of thoughts can help us find where shadows of the past are holding us back from ecstasy. If we are blocked in our mind, we will be blocked in our body as well. If we believe, because of what we have been taught, that feeling pleasure is bad, we must examine where these beliefs came from. Guilt has become a way of life in our culture, and it blocks us from feeling worthy of happiness and pleasure. Most of us need to work fervently to create new thought patterns that dissolve the guilty mindset we have. Practicing mindfulness can help us because it encourages less judgment of our feelings and thoughts and more self-acceptance. Be present to whatever is happening. Become a witness to your flow of thoughts and feelings. Approach your emotional and mental life like the sky—everything is just passing through like the weather. A greater level of awareness in every moment will come. When we free our mind, our outer senses will flourish; guilt will fade away, and we will begin feeling more ecstasy in our life.

What would feel good right now?

We can start exploring the territory of our inner life by asking questions and searching our memories and imagination. We can ask ourselves: What does ecstasy mean to me? What are my blocks to pleasure? What would feel good right now? What do I feel guilty about? What were the messages that I received as a child about pleasure? Our imagination can become the fertile soil for growing our courage and leading us toward a life of ecstasy. When we remember how we played as a child, we can rediscover our innocent nature, and we can play with the wonder and abandon of the young and free-spirited once again. We may discover that we need solitude to let go of our inhibitions and unlock our capacity to feel good. Or perhaps, as we embrace life as an ecstatic experience, we will be led back to the one we love with new eyes and a new passion.

However we go about it; one thing is sure: opening ourselves to ecstasy reveals a beautiful soul-light that shines from within. When we live an ecstatic life, we radiate a joy that draws other people to us. Our whole being becomes luminous. Feeling gloriously alive in our body, in our mind, and in our soul-life helps us see the divine in everything we experience.

Taste the sweet nectar of life, savor the beauty, drink liquid sunshine, belly laugh every day, and envision a joyful life. Pleasure in small things and simple moments can become our greatest joy. It is like winning the lottery every day. When we say yes to ecstasy, we are free to live and love wholeheartedly. Take a deep breath, open yourself to the divine, and prepare for ecstasy!

> *The question to ask yourself is:*
> *How can I fill my life with ecstasy?*

For Ecstasy

May the touch of your skin
feel the pleasure
of being gloriously
rapturously alive.

May swells of laughter
remind you
of the sweet gift
of friendship.

May the sound of your voice
be filled with
passion and desire
strength and song.

May the joy of ecstasy
find an open door in your heart
and rekindle in you
a raging fire of delight.

Julie Gohman, Ph.D.

How can I fill my life with ecstasy?

The Ninth Sacred Question

How can I fill my life with ecstasy?

The Tenth Sacred Question

What Do I Need To Flourish?

*I want to think again of dangerous and noble things.
I want to be light and frolicsome. I want to be
improbable beautiful and afraid of nothing,
as though I had wings.*
—Mary Oliver

Have you found true happiness? Are you thankful for each day that you've been given? Do you wake up and feel gloriously alive? If you are like me, some days you say an enthusiastic "yes," and some days you just want to bury your head and go back to sleep. But once we begin to look within, and learn how to listen to our heart and live from our soul, we will experience a radical transformation. We will get a glimpse of a greater vision, one where our happiness and creativity is a gift to the world. Therefore, when we nourish our true self, we fuel our ability to flourish—and when we flourish as women, the whole world flourishes with us.

When we live from our soul, and not the ego, our inner vision quietly guides us as we navigate ordinary reality. Our soul-voice is louder and easier to hear, and we begin questioning our assumptions about the nature of things, like happiness and what a successful life looks like. When our soul-voice is our constant companion, we can go beyond what appears on the surface. We come to understand that nothing outside ourselves makes us happy. Every woman must cultivate her own happiness. Happiness is not something we chase after or wait around for—happiness is something we create for ourselves. When we know this, our destiny beckons us to show up fully in our lives.

Our destiny beckons us to show up fully in our lives.

Women all over the world put happiness at the top of their list for what they want most in life. But if you are not as happy or as fulfilled as you would like to be, you're not alone. Many women would describe themselves as "moderately happy," but yet not flourishing. Flourishing takes happiness to a whole new level. We flourish when we make our well-being a priority.

According to the PERMA model of well-being by Dr. Martin Seligman, author of *Flourish*, there are five essential ingredients that create the foundation for flourishing. The first ingredient is positive emotions—meaning joy, hope, love, gratitude, etc. The second ingredient is engagement, meaning you find yourself blissfully absorbed in what you are doing. The third ingredient is positive relationships (loving and being loved). The fourth ingredient is meaning, which indicates the need to feel purposeful in life. The last ingredient is having a sense of accomplishment where you set goals and experience success. Use the following five questions to explore your current level of well-being and discover how you can begin flourishing.

Do you experience positive emotions in your daily life?

Positive emotion is a powerful tool for increasing resilience and life satisfaction. Ask yourself if you have positive emotions in your life: joy, gratitude, interest, serenity, hope, pride, amusement, inspiration and awe. If you feel you could use some help in this area, think about the people, places, and activities that make you come alive and bring a smile to your face. Try to develop a positive mindset by becoming more open to the good that is in your life and appreciating others. Feed your curiosity. Be kind to yourself. Create daily affirmations that are uplifting. And connect with what is real for you. Take one small step every day to nourish a more positive state of mind and heart.

Do you experience a state of flow regularly?

Flow is that state where time seems to stop, and you lose your sense of self. Your concentration is firmly rooted in the present moment, and your senses are wide open. That is engagement at it's best, and it feels creative, empowering, and really good. Engagement may come from your career, a hobby, or other activities that you enjoy. It may come when you are with friends, participating in sports, or working on a project that you feel passionate about. When are you in flow? Make time for personal interests, minimize distractions, and take concrete steps to decrease stress in your life. You will find yourself more engaged, and you are more likely to slip into a state of flow—and being in a state of flow leads to happiness.

Do you have positive relationships in your life?

Family, friends, colleagues, neighbors, anyone that you find positive and supportive and enjoy being around qualifies. Consider your work relationships. Look at your personal life. Make a commitment to spend time with family and friends that bring out the best in you. Reach out to those you would like to strengthen your bond with. Realize that good relationships take hard work and dedication. Look at all your relationships and decide which ones you want to preserve and which ones you want to release.

Do you have a sense of meaning and purpose?

Another way of looking at this is to answer the questions: What gets you out of bed in the morning? What are you living for? Finding meaning and purpose in what you are doing is important to your sense of well-being. This applies not only to your work life, but your personal life as well. If you lack meaning in your life, you may need to clarify your values and strengths. Create a personal mission statement that reflects what is important to you. Notice what you feel passionate about. Ultimately, living a meaningful life, in essence, is about being a part of something greater than you. Your sense of meaning and purpose may come from loving someone, caring for your children, volunteering in your community, or dedicating yourself wholeheartedly to your work. There are an infinite number of ways that you can live a meaningful life—what matters is that you find the path that is right for you.

What do you want to accomplish in your life?

Many women find it difficult to articulate what they want to accomplish in their life because they are busy just trying to get through the day. But take a moment to step back and reflect on your dreams, values and goals. Take the time to discover what you would love to do if you could do anything. What would a successful and meaning-filled future look like? If you were lying on your deathbed, what would you regret not doing? Only you can know when it is time to push yourself out of your comfort zone and try something new. Or maybe you need to pull back because you are over-committed and burned out. Find a balance that works for you.

There is a deep sense of rootedness in well-being. By being rooted in ourselves—in our true self—we gain the strength and fortitude to weather the storms of life. But more than this, we can direct and shape our life with conscious intention. When we choose to follow our heart, when we speak our truth, when we say yes to exciting new opportunities and experiences that enliven us, we become the powerful Creatress of our life. In other words, we flourish!

*Be kind and give yourself the time and
space to find your way to well-being.*

The journey to flourishing is like a pilgrimage through unforeseen places that enlarge and enrich your soul. As you regain a sense of wholeness and well-being, you return to the rhythm of your true self. You begin looking at your life in a refreshing new light. This new perspective will give you a great deal of peace about where you have been, acceptance of where you are now, and excitement about where you are going. Be kind and give yourself the time and space to find your way to well-being. Consider it an adventure of the soul that should not be rushed. It will unfold naturally as you give yourself what you need with loving kindness.

Finding wise mentors and guides is an important part of learning how to make healthy and nourishing choices as women. I look to other women who I trust, women who are smart, strong, and courageous. It is women like Dr. Christiane Northrup (the rock star of flourishing for women) who are on the leading edge. Think of a woman you admire, someone you would like to emulate, and let her be your guiding light. There are wise women all around us—remember that—and you will find your circle of support.

There are many good questions we can ask ourselves, such as: What do I feel positive about in my life? What relationships are draining me? Who is a source of support for me? What goals do I want to set for myself this year? Where do I want to be in ten years? How can I take one small step in the direction of my dreams? When do I feel creative and inspired? When do I find myself in a state of flow? What are my gifts? What makes my soul sing?

It is my hope that you will dive deep into your soul life as you begin wondering more about who you are as a woman, and what you need to flourish. The ripples of well-being will spread as you begin honoring your true self. Consider the following questions to help you get clear on what flourishing looks like right now for you. I suggest going through the questions with a journal to write in, and perhaps a trusted friend by your side.

What does the emotional landscape of my life look like?

We must listen to our emotions if we want to flourish. Our emotions are like a barometer, and they do not lie. When we feel stormy inside the world around us tends to look quite bleak. When we are filled with joy we notice the sunshine and fresh air, and everything seems wonderful. Emotions let us know whether we are going toward or away from our dreams. We will not always feel positive, but as a general rule when we feel joyful and optimistic, we know we are heading in the right direction.

Many of us were taught to suppress our emotions—a legacy that often shows up as bitterness, resentment, extra weight, and unhealthy habits. If we were not allowed to express ourselves naturally as children, we might need to learn how to release the emotions that are pent up inside us. When we release our emotions, it is like draining fluid from a deep wound so it can heal.

We also have to take full responsibility for our emotional life. What we feel is no one else's fault, no matter how justified we may be. We will never discover our power to choose joy and appreciation if we are always blaming other people. Our emotional life can be messy, complicated and painful at times. Choosing joy and appreciation may not seem possible. I invite you to honor the pain that you are feeling. Cry, punch pillows, scream, talk with someone who will deeply listen to you, journal, paint, run, sing, or just *be* with the feelings you have. Your well-being is anchored in experiencing all of your emotions, not just the pleasant ones. Welcome them all. Treat them tenderly, and know that every feeling is an invitation to wholeness.

Life is meant to be a pleasurable experience.

One easy way to assess the emotional landscape of your life is to think about how much pleasure you feel on a daily basis. Yes, that is right, pure pleasure that is all. Flourishing means experiencing generous portions of pleasure every day—whether from a child's smile, the aroma of chai in the morning, a lover's gentle touch or the beauty of a sunset. Life is meant to be a pleasurable experience.

How can I nourish my connection to the sacred?

Everyone lives an individual life, but we know we are part of a greater whole. Quantum physics tells us that separateness is an illusion. Our lives are enmeshed whether we see it or not. Becoming conscious of the sacred wholeness of life helps us to see beyond our small and selfish egos. Feeling connected to the sacred replenishes us, gives us strength and makes us resilient in times of hardship. Finding ways of connecting with the sacred on a regular basis helps us flourish.

Just as many rivers lead to the ocean, there are many ways to feel connected to the divine. Perhaps you feel closest to your source of power and wisdom when you meditate in silence, sing, write, dance, pray, play in the ocean, spend time in nature, giggle with children, explore your dreams, talk to angels, go to church, make love, or sit under a tree. All of these have worked for me during different times in my life. Open wide to the sacred and try something new.

There are many ways to connect with the sacred. We can all become spiritual seekers. Explore and get curious about what resonates for you. Ask yourself: What keeps my spiritual life alive? When do I feel a strong connection to the divine? Where do I feel the presence of God or my higher power? Develop daily practices that feed your soul. Find what's true for you.

How can I love myself more?

As women, we are biologically and socially wired to build our life around our connections to other people. Our relationships are at the center of our identity; they give our life meaning, and they affect the decisions we make every day. A secret to creating healthy, positive relationships is to create a foundation of self-love. When we love ourselves, we develop self-worth and self-respect, and this helps us set firm boundaries with others—our partner, children, family members, friends, and coworkers. Setting boundaries and standing up for ourselves is one of the best ways to improve our life and begin flourishing. We can be gracious, yet firm and direct, as we establish boundaries in areas of our life that are problematic. Personal power comes as we learn to take care of ourselves, though it sometimes feels uncomfortable at first. By loving ourselves we lay the foundation for healthy relationships, and we set ourselves up to flourish.

Personal power comes as we learn to take care of ourselves.

Without self-love, we feel unworthy. If we do not think we are worthy of being treated with respect, our relationships will be marked by irreverence. If we do not think we are worthy of being loved and accepted just as we are, our relationships will be filled with criticism. If we do not think we are capable of taking care of ourselves, our relationships will be codependent.

When we love ourselves, we listen to and honor the messages from our body. We trust our voice to speak the truth, and we honor our soul story. And we listen to our feminine intuition—the prickles on the back of our neck, the warmth or tightness in our abdomen, the rapid beat of our heart—guiding us to make wise decisions.

Loving ourselves takes practice. If we feel unworthy of love and acceptance because we aren't thin enough, good enough, pretty enough, rich enough, fill in the blank

_____ enough, we may need to work on erasing these beliefs and replacing them with messages that are more loving. Perhaps it would be helpful to work with a coach or therapist to examine where these limiting beliefs came from, and how to let go of them. We can learn to release these negative patterns, and forgive the past. We can learn how to love and accept ourselves just as we are. By taking small steps every day, with little acts of kindness and compassion, we will begin nurturing our true self. Positive changes will begin occurring as we move out of self-judgment and into self-love. We will see that loving ourselves is the key to flourishing in every area of our lives.

What do I believe?

Discovering our core beliefs is nothing less than revolutionary in our quest to flourish. If we want to be the best and happiest that we can be, we have to know ourselves deeply. Our core beliefs can show us how we want to live and where we want to be, and they can help us figure out what to do to get there. Living by our core beliefs enables us to act with self-determination, and live in harmony with our true self.

When we begin the process of sacred inquiry it is not unusual to find that our life is shaped more by our assumptions, rather than by our core beliefs. These assumptions often drag us down and limit our ability to flourish as women. We pick them up from our family of origin, our culture, the people around us, and especially from the media.

Many of us share some common assumptions that we mistake for the truth. The reality is that many of these assumptions obstruct us from living fearlessly and wholeheartedly. Three common ones that limit us as women are: we must sacrifice our life in order to please other people; we must put everyone else's needs first and our own needs last, and we cannot do, have, or be what we need and want. We must turn within and ask if we have fallen into the trap that too many women find themselves in—giving ourselves away until there is nothing left.

Learning how to listen to your heart and get what you need to be happy while still taking care of others is possible, but you must be brave. Have faith, and trust that you will find creative ways of saying yes to yourself without neglecting the ones you love. As you begin to flourish you will find that your energy and enthusiasm will grow by leaps and bounds. You are living from your center and there will come to be a healthy balance between what you are giving and what you are receiving.

Where is my circle?

Every woman needs a circle of support in order to flourish. Having people who love, encourage, and believe in you gives you the confidence to do great things. Every woman needs safe places, and safe people, to reflect the beauty and goodness of her true self. Your circle of support will help you to find the strength and courage to live and thrive through all the joys and sorrows of life.

If we isolate ourselves from the warmth and caring of others, we lose out on the important connections that are essential to our sense of well-being and happiness. But when we engage with our circle of support we are surrounded in love, and secret places inside of us are nourished. A circle of support often makes the difference between getting lost in the chaos of life and finding our way back home to our true self.

It is also important to remember that reaching out to someone who can listen and guide us during times of crisis is a sign of courage, not weakness. If we need more support than we have, we can widen the circle. We can find someone—a therapist, life coach, or spiritual counselor—who can help us reassess our life and make positive changes. Or we may find that a twelve-step support group is what we need most. There is no shame in getting help when we need it. In fact, it is often the healthiest thing we can do to make life better.

Am I ready to become a curious explorer?

If you asked Todd Kashdan, Ph.D. what the central ingredient is to living a rich and meaningful life he would say "curiosity." In his book *Curious? Discover the Missing Ingredient to a Fulfilling Life* he suggests that while curiosity may seem like a simple concept, it is actually a complex phenomenon that plays a critical role in our ability to pursue a meaningful life.

While curiosity helps us to discover what makes us sizzle with excitement, it goes far deeper than that. Kashdan teaches that curiosity goes beyond novelty and is more about how we relate to our thoughts and feelings, and how we pay attention to what is happening in the present. Curiosity becomes a pathway to being fully engaged and alive to our experiences. It energizes us and puts us into a receptive frame of mind. Being open and receptive leads to more spontaneity and variety in life. A variety of interesting experiences add that spice and zest to an otherwise familiar and often mundane road.

Without curiosity we lack the motivation to explore, discover and grow. At the most fundamental level, curiosity drives us to seek out new and uncertain experiences. Curiosity moves us in the direction of actively creating our lives. Instead of becoming complacent about our relationships, careers, beliefs, values, and personal development we can learn to infuse a large dose of wonder and curiosity—and wake ourselves up.

Courage mixed with curiosity leads to important questions such as: Does my voice matter in this relationship? Is this what I really want? What do I need to feel loved? Am I spending my time and money in ways that feel purposeful? How can I make healthy changes in my life? Do I need to get some help? What are my challenges right now as a woman, as a mother, as a partner or wife? What are my wishes for this year? What is my long-range vision for the future? What makes me laugh? What makes me cry? We need to keep asking questions with an open heart that is filled with hope, determination, and the confidence that we can find our way to a radiant and flourishing life if we don't give up and we don't give in.

What do I *really* want?

It takes courage to follow your heart and create what you really want in your life. Elizabeth Gilbert, best-selling author of *Eat, Pray, Love,* advocates saying it this way, "What do I really, really, really want?" It takes three "really's" to get down beneath all the stuff we think we want. Underneath the surface, there is actually a feeling that you want. Do you want good health? The feeling you crave may be vitality, mobility, and vibrancy. Do you want financial prosperity?

The feeling you are after may be freedom, choice, and personal power. Whatever it is that you want, dig deep to find the feelings underneath it. With an awareness of the emotional underpinnings of what you want, you can begin creating goals more consciously, and taking steps to achieve your dreams. It takes strength and determination to set goals and accomplish what you set out to do. To flourish, you must dwell on the possibilities for your life—pursuing your desires, dreams, passions, and goals—and not dwell on your limitations.

Many of us have been taught that we cannot have what we *really* want. We are filled with self-doubt and so we hesitate. For many reasons, biology, upbringing, and society, confidence does not come easy to most women. Afraid we might fail; we do not even try. Instead, we must begin to believe in our ability to be successful, and we must be willing to take action. As the feminist activist Audre Lorde said, when we dare to be powerful, to use our strength in service to our vision, then it becomes less and less important whether we are afraid.

*The wisdom that comes from our heart
will tell us what we need to flourish.*

Taking action requires courage, and can lead to both success and failure—there are no guarantees. But when you make the choice to go for it, to take a risk, you will inevitably build your confidence muscles. Experiment, explore, discover who you are and what you want by trying things. Tune into the messages from your body, and the wisdom from your heart to guide you toward what is meaningful. What you want may change and that's okay. You are becoming the *expert* of your own life.

You can start uncovering your passions and desires by noticing what naturally enlivens you. It does not have to be complicated or expensive; it may be the simple things in your daily life that give you the best clues. Perhaps you notice how good it feels to take a walk every morning. Maybe you enjoy volunteering in your community, learning about world politics, planting a garden, caring for animals, or writing poetry. Notice what interests you, what feels good, and where you feel energized. Ask yourself: what do I love about this?

When we pay attention to the little pleasures that we experience throughout the day, it is easier to hear the voice from our soul that tells us what we really want to do, achieve, and create. Listening to our innermost desires and our most cherished dreams allows us to begin taking baby steps toward achieving them.

Flourishing begins with knowing yourself and showing love to yourself. It means honoring your journey as a woman. Every woman deserves a life that she loves. You deserve to feel radiantly alive. Right now, wherever you find yourself, is a good time to start moving in the direction of joy and bliss. Right now is the perfect time to begin creating more positive relationships in your life. Right now is the best time to discover your purpose. Right now is the time for you to accomplish great things.

The question to ask yourself is: What do I need to flourish?

For a Radiant Life

May you listen deeply
to the wisdom of your body
and stand in awe
at the beauty and wonder
of your feminine form.

May you be filled
with the flames
of passion and pleasure
and live to the full
all that you have been given.

May you be blessed
with the treasure
of a heart that sees
the circle of love
that unites us.

May you hear the echoes
of your deepest desires
on the waves of pure possibility
as you step into the light
and radiantly flourish.

Julie Gohman, Ph.D.

What do I need to flourish?

The Tenth Sacred Question

What do I need to flourish?

Epilogue:
The Most Powerful Question of all

What Am I Grateful For?

> *'Thank you' is the best prayer that anyone could say...*
> *Thank you expresses extreme gratitude, humility,*
> *understanding.*
> —Alice Walker

A book of sacred questions would not be complete without mentioning what is perhaps the most powerful question we can ask ourselves: What am I grateful for? Gratitude changes everything; it transforms our perception of reality so much that it changes the world we see. Every woman can use the power of gratitude to reach for a life that is filled with beauty and joy and abundance.

Being grateful is based on knowing deep in our heart that life is for us, not against us. When we commit to expressing gratitude every day, our lives take on a golden hue. What we used to take for granted—the air we breathe, someone who loves us, good health, food to eat, and just being alive—becomes a divine gift. Gratitude is a simple, but powerful practice that helps us weave a consciousness and destiny that is filled with light and love.

Julie Gohman, Ph.D.

We can live our days focused on what we find wrong in our life—what is missing and what we do not like—or we can dwell on the good, true, and beautiful. We must ultimately realize that what we focus on affects the state of our mind and heart, for better or worse. When we understand how our own thoughts shape our experiences, we move away from being a victim of circumstance, and toward being the powerful creator of our life. We learn to take responsibility for our mental activity knowing that we are always at choice. In every moment we get to choose whether we will dwell on thoughts of peace, prosperity, love, and gratitude—or not.

All we are, and all we have is a gift.

Practicing gratitude becomes a way of life. It means living in humility, generosity, and with an awareness of the precious nature of the time we've been given. When we inhabit this world knowing that we are all part of the divine, we see the beauty of the human spirit and the timeless wisdom of nature. Nothing helps us to move beyond our small self—our ego—more than looking around in the spirit of awe and gratitude. Our life may not be easy, but gratitude can shift our perspective in an instant. All we are, and all we have is a gift.

Gratitude comes from the heart, and it is felt in the body as pure joy, pure peace. It is that feeling we get when we are in a sacred place, or making love, or holding a child, or feeling the sunshine on our face. The beauty of that moment floods our being, overwhelms our senses, leaves us breathless, in tears, and filled with reverence for all that is. Deep gratitude moves us, brings us to our knees, and fills our soul with radical humility.

Gratitude and suffering

It is not easy to be grateful in the midst of suffering, but it can be done. When we practice gratitude as a way of life, we are always searching for things to be grateful for. Whatever shows up on our path—however difficult or unpleasant it may be—gives us the opportunity to practice unconditional gratitude. Even situations that are painful, disappointing and frustrating can become an exercise of awareness—to be able to see the spiritual gifts in all our experiences. Through unconditional gratitude, we can see that everything is here to bless us.

Everything is here to bless us.

Make no mistake; I am not suggesting that we should ever be grateful for oppressive or bad situations. For example, if we are in a bad relationship, we can be grateful for the fact that we have two legs that can walk right on out of there. We can be grateful for the wisdom and insight we have gained from our experiences, even the painful ones. Each time we make a mistake, we can reflect on it, forgive ourselves, and learn from it, and then we can go forward in our lives stronger and wiser.

Gratitude can be practiced in even the most inhumane, challenging, and unjust circumstances. Harriet Tubman was born into slavery in 1822. As a child Tubman was lashed, beaten, and even sustained a head injury from an abusive master that caused her seizures for the rest of her life. As a young woman, Harriet, or "Minty" as she was affectionately called, married a free man but remained a slave. Soon after, she began to plan her escape. In 1849, she set out on foot by herself, hiding in marshes and woods during the day and traveling during the night to avoid the slave catchers. With the help of the Underground Railroad, Harriet arrived in

Pennsylvania and found herself a free woman. That however was just the beginning for Harriet. She wanted to help guide other slaves to freedom as well. She became a conductor of the Underground Railroad and began making trips back to Maryland to help family members and friends escape slavery. Harriet helped so many people find their way to freedom that she was given the name "Moses," like the prophet in the Book of Exodus, who led the Hebrews out of Egypt.

Harriet encountered many struggles in her lifetime, more than most of us could ever imagine, but she never let them stop her from living with the courage and conviction that comes from a grateful and generous heart. Many years after she first arrived in Philadelphia she recalled the wonder and relief that filled her being, knowing she was a free woman. She said, "I looked at my hands to see if I was the same person. There was such a glory over everything. The sun came up like gold through the trees, and I felt like I was in heaven." When we have that kind of deeply felt gratitude in our heart, we are in a heaven of our own making, a freedom that breaks through all of our suffering. Harriet's legacy continues to inspire us. She said, "Every great dream begins with a dreamer. Always remember, you have within you the strength, the patience, and the passion to reach for the stars, to change the world."

> *"You have within you the strength,*
> *the patience, and the passion*
> *to reach for the stars,*
> *to change the world."*

Another story comes from the Rwandan Genocide that occurred in the mid-1990's and a brave young woman

Epilogue: The Most Powerful Question of all

named Immaculée Ilibagiza. In her book, *Left to Tell: Discovering God Amidst the Rwandan Holocaust*, she tells her personal story of surviving the genocide by hiding in a tiny, cramped bathroom for 91 days with seven other women. Outside the bathroom door were hundreds of machete-wielding killers hunting for any person who was a Tutsi, one of the ethnic groups living in Rwanda. Prior to the genocide, Immaculée grew up in a happy village where people respected and cared for one another. When the genocide began, suddenly all that mattered was if you were a "Hutu" or a "Tutsi." Immaculée happened to be a Tutsi, and for that she became a target for angry extremists who intended to eradicate the country of all Tutsi's.

For 91 days, Immaculée trembled in fear as she hid in the tiny bathroom of a pastor's house. The whole time, Immaculée never stopped praying to God. The mental anguish was intense. She was filled with worry and fear for her family, not knowing if they were dead or alive, and she never knew when the killers would come back to search the pastor's house yet again. Immaculée found that the only thing that helped ease her anxiety was prayer. And she always began with devotions of thanksgiving. "My first prayer was always to thank God that the pastor's home had been built so it could shelter us during the genocide. Then I thanked him for having the architect design the house with an extra bathroom, and for prompting the pastor to buy a wardrobe of exactly the right dimensions to conceal our hiding place."

Prayer became Immaculée's armor that she wrapped tightly around her heart. She prayed to let go of her anger against the killers, and found pity for them instead. She asked God to forgive their sins and turn their souls toward the light. And when the French finally came to Rwanda to help the Tutsi's, and the genocide ended, she whispered "Thank you God." Now, Immaculée speaks to people all over the world about what happened to her in Rwanda. She wrote, "God saved my soul and spared my life for a reason: He left me to tell my story to others and show as many people as possible the healing power of His love and forgiveness."

Gratitude and forgiveness

If we want to have peace, joy, and love—the fruits of the spirit—in our life, we must open ourselves to the power of forgiveness. Practicing gratitude puts us on the path. When we intentionally practice gratitude we feel the winds of grace moving through our life. We begin to see that it is completely within our power to live through all our experiences. As illogical as it may sound, when we forgive, and let go of our blame, guilt, and judgment, we are really giving ourselves a gift, not letting the other person off the hook. Forgiveness and gratitude are sisters that free us from the prison of hatred and self-pity.

Something sacred is waiting to be seen in every moment.

Practicing gratitude is a lot like meditation. We stop, breathe, and observe our thoughts without judging them. We make a conscious choice to turn our mind to the light, and to reach for the best in every moment. We let go of anger, resentment, and bitterness and embrace forgiveness. Even if we cannot think of anything to be grateful for, our intention to practice gratitude will eventually lead to a shift in our consciousness. We will begin seeing things more positively.

Something sacred is waiting to be seen in every moment. When we look for something to be grateful for, we are uplifted. It is impossible to be in a state of pessimism and gratitude at the same time. Gratitude shifts us from negativity to positivity. It becomes the bridge between where we are and where we want to be. It is much easier to show gratitude in even the harshest circumstances when we commit to focusing on the good in life, even if all we can say is "At least I am still breathing." As Helen Keller said, "Keep your face to the sunshine and you cannot see the shadows."

Gratitude and abundance

Abundance is not just about how much money we have. We can feel the spirit of gratitude and abundance whether we have five dollars in our pocket or five million in the bank. I have met millionaires who feel like beggars, and I know people who have very little (material possessions) but feel richly blessed. When our soul is attuned to what is good, true, and beautiful, we are living in gratitude. We are open to the unlimited abundance that exists everywhere, and the shape of our life reflects this. Rather than bemoaning our fate, we find and celebrate the good. We do not waste our time complaining, but rather we give praise in the spirit of gratitude.

*Let your spirit of gratitude overflow
into blessings all around you.*

There is symmetry between our inner life of thoughts and the form of our outer world. When we take responsibility for *how* we see the world, we find out very quickly that it determines *what* we see as well. As we grow in awareness about how powerful our mind is, we realize that we see the world not as it is, but as we are. We are like crystals that create different colors and patterns depending on the angle of our reflection. When we look around in awe and wonder and gratitude, we feel more abundant, and we naturally become more generous. As we affirm our prosperity, we share what we have more graciously, knowing in our heart that life's goodness is ever present.

The abundance you feel in your mind and heart will manifest into all your experiences. Let your spirit of gratitude overflow into blessings all around you. Follow the advice from Mother Theresa, who said, "Spread love everywhere you go. Let no one ever come to you without leaving happier." An attitude of gratitude touches your life with abundance and allows you to share it joyfully with others. Make your prayer in each moment one that begins with "thank you" and your life will be filled with more good than you could imagine.

Tried and True Gratitude Practices From Me to You

Before you get out of bed in the morning, find something to be grateful for. Perhaps it is a soft pillow beneath your head, the person lying next to you, your healthy body, a new day, whatever comes to you as you wake up. Whisper it quietly, feel it in your heart, sing it soulfully, shout it out loud and wake everyone in the house—it's up to you—just do it. Set your alarm five minutes early and begin your day in the spirit of gratitude and abundance.

Be on the lookout for people and situations to be thankful for. As my grandma used to say, "Count your blessings." The more we seize opportunities to say "thank you," the more we will find that life is full of things to be grateful for.

Begin every email message with appreciation, recognition, and gratitude. Everyone needs to know that they count, that someone appreciates what they are doing—let that person be you, and let your messages be uplifting to others.

Develop a daily routine of expressing your gratitude out loud while driving, walking, or even taking a shower. It might feel strange at first, but give it a try. My kids think I'm silly when I'm driving them to school in the morning and singing about all the things I am thankful for—but by the time we arrive at school we all feel more joyful for the new day, for our life, and for each other. If someone like me, a person who can't carry a tune to save her soul, can do this—so can you!

Write in a gratitude journal every day—and read through it often. Find a special time when you have a few moments to yourself and reflect on all the good things in your life. Writing in a gratitude journal is also a practice that can be shared with your children or family.

Be willing to receive. Open your arms and accept gifts when they come into your life instead of pushing them away. Know you are worthy of every good thing.

Create a family tradition of sharing what you are grateful for around the dinner table every night. Let your kitchen be transformed into your very own Café Gratitude. Take a cue from the successful California chain that believes in the power of affirmations. Serve up healthy dishes such as "I Am Inspired," "I Am Abundant," "I Am Thriving," and "I Am Satisfied." This is a great way to put your attention on what you wish to create in your life.

Send the special people in your life a handwritten letter (and maybe a little gift too), telling them how much you love and appreciate them. It may be a teacher from your childhood, a mentor who helped you find your way, a dear auntie, or a close friend. Take the time to show gratitude to the people who have believed in you, supported you, and helped you become who you are.

Contemplate the blessings that have come from the most difficult situations you have experienced in life. Find gratitude in your heart for how much you have grown, for the strength you have developed, and for your resilient nature.

Show love and gratitude to yourself for the beautiful and amazing woman that you are. Do as Louise Hay, author of *You Can Heal Your Life*, teaches: look in the mirror and say, "I love you, I really, really love you." It may feel awkward at first, but just do it—it is a powerful affirmation that works magic.

Melody Beattie said this about gratitude, "Gratitude unlocks the fullness of life. It turns what we have into enough, and more. It turns denial into acceptance, chaos to order, confusion to clarity. It can turn a meal into a feast, a house into a home, a stranger into a friend. Gratitude makes sense of our past, brings peace for today and creates a vision for tomorrow."

The question to ask yourself is: What am I grateful for?

For Gratitude

*I wake up today
blessed by all things
breath of life
a soul filled with love
joy in my heart.*

*I arise today
blessed with hope
surrounded by beauty
filled with reverence
for this moment in time.*

*I live this day
blessed by compassion
nourished by grace
generous in spirit
and grateful for all that is.*

Julie Gohman, Ph.D.

What am I grateful for?

Epilogue: The Most Powerful Question of all

What am I grateful for?

Suggested Reading List

Anderson, Rosemarie. *Celtic Oracles: A New System for Spiritual Growth and Divination.* New York: Three Rivers Press, 2000.

Anderson, R. (2006). Defining and measuring body intelligence: Introducing the Body Intelligence Scale. *The Humanistic Psychologist,* 34(4), 357-367.

Angelou, Maya. *And Still I Rise.* New York: Random House, 1978.

Armstrong, Karen. *A history of God: The 4,000-year quest of Judaism, Christianity and Islam.* New York: Ballantine, 1993.

Baring, Anne & Cashford, Jules. *The Myth of the Goddess: Evolution of an Image.* New York: Penguin, 1991.

Barks, Coleman (translator). *The Essential Rumi.* New York: HarperOne, 2004.

Bolen, Jean Shinoda. *Goddesses in Everywoman.* New York: Harper Perennial, 1984.

Rowe, Nancy Mangano. Listening Through the Body. In: *The Wisdom of Listening* by Mark Brady. Somerville, MA: Wisdom, 2003.

Braiker, Harriet B. *The Disease to Please: Curing the People-pleasing Syndrome*. New York: McGraw-Hill, 2001.

Brown, Brené. Daring Greatly: *How the Courage to be Vulnerable Transforms the way we Live, Love, Parent, and Lead*. New York: Gotham, 2012.

Buber, Martin. *I and Thou*. New York: Touchstone, 1970.

Buscalia, Leo. *Love*. Thorofare, NJ: Charles B. Slack, Inc., 1972.

Cameron, Julia. *The Artist's Way: A Spiritual Path to Higher Creativity*. New York: Jeremy P. Tarcher/Putnam, 2002.

Campbell, Joseph. *Pathways to bliss: Mythology and Personal Transformation*. Novato, CA: New World Library, 2004.

Carrellas, Barbara. *Ecstasy is Necessary: A Practical Guide*. New York: Hay House, 2012.

Christ, Carol P. Why Women Need the Goddess: Phenomenological, Psychological, and Political Reflections. In *Womanspirit Rising: A Feminist Reader in Religion* by Carol P. Christ & Judith Plaskow. New York: HarperSanFrancisco, 1992.

Diamant, Anita. *The Red Tent*. New York: Picador, 1997.

Dickinson, Emily. *The Poems of Emily Dickinson*. Cambridge, MA: Belknap Press, 2005.

Eisler, Riane. *Sacred pleasure: Sex, Myth, and the Politics of the Body – New Paths to Power and Love*. New York: HarperCollins, 1996.

Eknath Easwaran (Ed.). *The Bhagavad Gita*. Canada: Nilgiri Press, 2007.

Estés, Clarissa Pinkola. *Women Who Run With the Wolves*. New York: Ballantine, 1996.

Ford, Arielle. *Wabi Sabi Love: The Ancient Art of Finding Perfect Love in Imperfect Relationships*. New York: HarperCollins, 2012.

Gawain, Shakti. *Creative Visualization: Use the Power of Your Imagination to Create What You Want in Your Life*. Novato, CA: New World Library, 2002.

Gilbert, Elizabeth. *Eat, Pray. Love: One Woman's Search for Everything Across Italy, India and Indonesia*. New York: Penguin, 2007.

Hay, Louise L. *You Can Heal Your Life*. Carlsbad, CA: Hay House, 1999.

Hendricks, Gay. *Five wishes: How Answering One Simple Question can Make Your Dreams Come True*. Novato, CA: New World Library, 2007.

Hicks, Esther & Jerry. *Ask and It Is Given: Learning to Manifest Your Desires*. New York: Hay House, 2004.

Hopkins, Emma Curtis. *Scientific Christian mental practice.* New York: DeVorss, 1974.

Ilibagiza, Immaculée. *Left to Tell: Discovering God Amidst the Rwandan Holocaust.* New York: Hay House, 2006.

Jung, Carl. *Memories, Dreams, Reflections.* Ed. Aniela Jaffe. New York: Vintage, 1989.

Kashdan, Todd. Ph.D. *Curious? Discover the Missing Ingredient to a Fulfilling Life.* New York: Harper Perennial, 2010.

Keller, Helen. *The World I Live in and Optimism: A Collection of Essays.* Mineola, New York: Dover, 2012.

Knaster, Mirka. *Discovering the Body's Wisdom.* New York: Bantam, 1996.

Leidenfrost, Isadora Gabrielle. *Things We Do Not Talk About: Women's Stories From The Red Tent* (film). www.redtenttemplemovement.com

Lesser, Elizabeth. *The Seeker's Guide: Making Your Life a Spiritual Adventure.* New York: Villard, 1999.

Miller, Jean Baker. *Toward a new psychology of women. Boston, MA: Beacon Press, 1986.*

Myers, Linda. *The Power of Memoir: How to Write Your Healing Story.* San Francisco, CA: Jossey-Bass.

Naparstek, Belleruth. *Your Sixth Sense: Awakening Your Psychic Potential.* New York: HarperSanFrancisco, 1997.

Neff, Kristin. *Self-Compassion: The Proven Power of Being Kind to Yourself.* New York: HarperCollins, 2011.

Nhat Hanh, Thích. *The Miracle of Mindfulness: An Introduction to the Practice of meditation.* Boston, MA: Beacon Press, 1999.

Northrup, Christiane. *Women's Bodies, Women's Wisdom: Creating Physical and Emotional Healing.* New York: Bantam, 2010.

Northrup, Christiane and Schulz, Mona Lisa. *Intuitive Listening: How Intuition Talks Through Your Body.* Carlsbad: Hay House, 2006. Audio CD.

O'Donohue, John. *Anam Cara: A Book of Celtic Wisdom.* New York: Cliff Street, 1997.

Ogden, Gina. *The Heart and Soul of Sex: Exploring the Sexual Mysteries.* Boston, MA: Trumpeter, 2006.

Ogden, Gina. *The Return of Desire: A Guide to Rediscovering Your Sexual Passion.* Boston: Trumpeter, 2008.

Oliver, Mary. *Owls and Other Fantasies: Poems and Essays.* Boston, MA: Beacon Press, 2003.

Orloff, Judith. *Positive Energy: 10 Extraordinary Prescriptions for Transforming Fatigue, Stress and Fear into Vibrance, Strength, and Love.* New York: Three Rivers, 2004.

Raab, Diane. *Healing with Words: A Writer's Cancer Journey.* Ann Arbor, MI: Loving Healing Press.

Rilke, Raniner Maria. *The Selected Poetry of Rainer Maria Rilke.* Ed. and Trans. Stephen Mitchell. New York: Vintage, 1989.

Ross, Elisabeth Kübler & David Kessler. *Life Lessons: Two Experts on Death and Dying Teach Us About the Mysteries of Life & Living.* New York: Simon & Schuster, 2000.

Ruumet, Hillevi. *Pathways of the Soul: Exploring the Human Journey.* Victoria, BC, Canada: Trafford, 2006.

Salzberg, Sharon. Real Happiness: The Power of Meditation. New York: Workman, 2011.

Sarton, May. May Sarton: Collected Poems 1930-1993. New York: W.W. Norton, 1993.

Schulz, Mona Lisa. *Awakening Intuition: Using Your Mind-Body Network for Insight and Healing.* New York: Three Rivers Press, 1998.

Seligman, Martin E.P. *Flourish: A Visionary New Understanding of Happiness and Well-being.* New York: Free Press, 2011.

The Mother & Sri Aurobindo. *Living Within: Yoga Approach to Psychological Health & Growth.* San Francisco, CA: Institute of Integral Psychology, 1987.

Starhawk. *Dreaming the Dark: Magic, Sex, and Politics.* Boston, MA: Beacon Press, 1982.

Starhawk. *The Spiral Dance: A Rebirth of the Ancient Religion of the Goddess.* New York, HarperOne, 1989.

Thích Nhat Hanh. *The Miracle of Mindfulness.* Boston, MA: Beacon Press, 1987.

Walker, Alice. *Hard Times Require Furious Dancing: New Poems.* Novato, CA: New World Library, 2010.

Walker, Barbara. *The Women's Encyclopedia of Myths and Secrets.* New York: HarperCollins, 1983.

Williamson, Marianne. *Reflections on the Principles of a "Course in Miracles"* New York: HarperCollins, 1996.

Winqvist, Agneta Nyholm. *Wabi Sabi: Timeless Wisdom for a Stress-free Life.* New York: Skyhorse, 2012.

Woodman, Marion. *Leaving my Father's House: A Journey to Conscious Femininity.* Boston, MA: Shambhala, 1992.

About Julie Gohman

Julie Gohman Ph.D. is a writer and adjunct professor at St. Cloud State University in Minnesota, where she teaches *Psychology of Women*. She received her doctorate in Psychology from Sofia University in California, and is a member of the Society for Humanistic Psychology, and the Association for Transpersonal Psychology. She presents regionally, nationally, and internationally about women's development, motherhood, feminine spirituality, and practices of inquiry. She lives in Minnesota with her husband and two sons. For more information go to www.juliegohman.com

www.ingramcontent.com/pod-product-compliance
Lightning Source LLC
Chambersburg PA
CBHW060151050426
42446CB00013B/2765